WORLD HISTORY

The Rwandan Genocide

Don Nardo

LUCENT BOOKS

A part of Gale, Cengage Learning

GALE
CENGAGE Learning

Detroit • New York • San Francisco • New Haven, Conn • Waterville, Maine • London

GALE
CENGAGE Learning

LIBRARY OF CONGRESS CATALOGING-IN-PUBLICATION DATA

Nardo, Don, 1947-
 The Rwandan genocide / by Don Nardo.
    p. cm. -- (World history)
 Includes bibliographical references and index.
 ISBN 978-1-4205-0567-2 (hardcover)
 1. Genocide--Rwanda--History--20th century--Juvenile literature.
 2. Ethnic conflict--Rwanda--History--20th century--Juvenile literature.
 3. Rwanda--History--Civil War, 1994--Juvenile literature. 4. Rwanda--
 Ethnic relations--History--20th century--Juvenile literature. I. Title.
  DT450.435.N27 2011
  967.57104'31--dc22
                                                                          2010039533

Lucent Books
27500 Drake Rd.
Farmington Hills, MI 48331

ISBN-13: 978-1-4205-0567-2
ISBN-10: 1-4205-0567-X

Printed in the United States of America
1 2 3 4 5 6 7 15 14 13 12 11

Printed by Bang Printing, Brainerd, MN, 1st Ptg., 03/2011

Contents

Foreword

Each year, on the first day of school, nearly every history teacher faces the task of explaining why his or her students should study history. Many reasons have been given. One is that lessons exist in the past from which contemporary society can benefit and learn. Another is that exploration of the past allows us to see the origins of our customs, ideas, and institutions. Concepts such as democracy, ethnic conflict, or even things as trivial as fashion or mores, have historical roots.

Reasons such as these impress few students, however. If anything, these explanations seem remote and dull to young minds. Yet history is anything but dull. And therein lies what is perhaps the most compelling reason for studying history: History is filled with great stories. The classic themes of literature and drama—love and sacrifice, hatred and revenge, injustice and betrayal, adversity and overcoming adversity—fill the pages of history books, feeding the imagination as well as any of the great works of fiction do.

The story of the Children's Crusade, for example, is one of the most tragic in history. In 1212 Crusader fever hit Europe. A call went out from the pope that all good Christians should journey to Jerusalem to drive out the hated Muslims and return the city to Christian control. Heeding the call, thousands of children made the journey. Parents bravely allowed many children to go, and entire communities were inspired by the faith of these small Crusaders. Unfortunately, many boarded ships were captained by slave traders, who enthusiastically sold the children into slavery as soon as they arrived at their destination. Thousands died from disease, exposure, and starvation on the long march across Europe to the Mediterranean Sea. Others perished at sea.

Another story, from a modern and more familiar place, offers a soul-wrenching view of personal humiliation but also the ability to rise above it. Hatsuye Egami was one of 110,000 Japanese Americans sent to internment camps during World War II. "Since yesterday we Japanese have ceased to be human beings," he wrote in his diary. "We are numbers. We are no longer Egamis, but the number 23324. A tag with that number is on every trunk, suitcase and bag. Tags, also, on our breasts." Despite such dehumanizing treatment, most internees worked hard to control their bitterness. They created workable communities inside the camps and demonstrated again and again their loyalty as Americans.

These are but two of the many stories from history that can be found in the pages of the Lucent Books World History series. All World History titles rely on sound research and verifiable evidence, and all give students a clear sense of time, place, and chronology through maps and timelines as well as text.

All titles include a wide range of authoritative perspectives that demonstrate the complexity of historical interpretation and sharpen the reader's critical thinking skills. Formally documented quotations and annotated bibliographies enable students to locate and evaluate sources, often instantaneously via the Internet, and serve as valuable tools for further research and debate.

Finally, Lucent's World History titles present rousing good stories, featuring vivid primary source quotations drawn from unique, sometimes obscure sources such as diaries, public records, and contemporary chronicles. In this way, the voices of participants and witnesses as well as important biographers and historians bring the study of history to life. As we are caught up in the lives of others, we are reminded that we too are characters in the ongoing human saga, and we are better prepared for our own roles.

Important Dates at the Time

ca. 1300–1450
The Kingdom of Rwanda is formed along the shores of Lake Muhazi, in east-central Africa.

1884
Europe's leading powers meet in Berlin, Germany, and carve up most of Africa; Rwanda becomes a German colony.

1776
Britain's thirteen North American colonies rebel and establish the United States of America.

1912
A huge, new luxury liner, the RMS *Titanic*, sinks in the North Atlantic, and 1,517 passengers and crew die.

1962
In the midst of a large-scale African independence movement, Belgium grants self-rule to Rwanda.

1500	1800	1900	1940	1980

1487
Portuguese navigator Bartolomeu Dias is the first European to reach the Cape of Good Hope, in southern Africa.

1914–1918
Nations around the world engage in World War I.

1916
While engaged in World War I, Belgium seizes control of Rwanda from Germany.

1939–1945
Nations around the world engage in World War II.

1973
Rwandan army officer Juvénal Habyarimana becomes dictatorial ruler of Rwanda.

of the Rwandan Genocide

1980
Ronald Reagan becomes president of the United States.

1993
The RPF and Habyarimana's government reach an agreement, called the Arusha Accords.

1990
Armed members of the RPF invade Rwanda from the north.

1996
The United Nations sets up the International Criminal Tribunal for Rwanda to convict the genocide's worst offenders.

2001
Terrorists hijack four airliners in the United States, and the planes crash into the World Trade Center in New York, the Pentagon in Maryland, and a field in Pennsylvania, killing nearly four thousand people.

| 1985 | 1990 | 1995 | 2000 | 2005 |

1987
The Rwandan Patriotic Front (RPF) is established.

1991
U.S.-led allied forces enter Iraq to free the nation of Kuwait, recently seized by Iraqi dictator Saddam Hussein.

1998
U.S. president Bill Clinton admits that his country did not do enough to help stop the mass murders in Rwanda.

1994
Juvénal Habyarimana is assassinated, igniting a large-scale genocide and hundreds of thousands of Rwandans are killed.

2010
In Rwanda, trials of the genocide's perpetrators continue.

A Crime Like No Other

In 1994 thousands of young men, most armed with machetes (large knife-like blades) and various farm implements, roamed through the villages and countryside of the small central African nation of Rwanda. Urged on by government officials and state-sponsored radio broadcasts, the young men formed death squads. In a shocking display of barbarity and cruelty, they murdered their neighbors, strangers, and in some cases even members of their own families. Most of the victims belonged to an ethnic group different from that of the killers. Supposedly the victims deserved to be killed because they posed a threat to the country. In this manner, hundreds of thousands of people were hacked to death or otherwise slain in a little more than three months.

Eventually the killings stopped and order was restored in Rwanda. Hearing what had occurred there, people around the world were horrified and much was said and written about what happened. It did not take long for the killings to be labeled as genocide. Legal and law enforcement experts say that genocide is a crime like no other. It is more horrendous and unspeakable than the murder of an individual or even ordinary mass murder, because genocide is an attempt to wipe out an entire group, or category, of people, to eliminate their existence forever.

Coining a New Term

When people around the world heard about the Rwandan genocide, most of them did not know that the term *genocide* is relatively new. Large-scale killings had occurred in the past, of course. They have, in fact, occurred throughout recorded history. But they had been given many and diverse labels, among them "killing spree," "massacre," "mass murder," "slaughter of innocents," and so forth.

Nazi Germany, led by its brutal dictator, Adolf Hitler, systematically murdered more than 6 million Jews, in many instances by herding them into large gas chambers, during World War II (1939-1945). (Some scholars define the Holocaust more expansively to cover the Nazis' attempted extermination of other groups, including Gypsies, handicapped

Human bones and skulls lie in a pile at the Nazi concentration camp in Majdanek, Poland, in 1944. These Nazi "crimes against humanity" would become known as genocide.

individuals, and homosexuals. The death toll of the Holocaust is estimated to be between 11 and 17 million people when these groups are included.)

Toward the end of the war, when the Allies (the nations fighting Germany in the war) discovered the scope of these Nazi mass murders, they also realized something else: No word existed that described such an immense and well-planned effort to completely wipe out entire groups of people. Indeed, Britain's leader at the time, Prime Minister Winston Churchill, called it "a crime with no name."[1] Churchill was acknowledging that the Nazis' slaughter of Jews and other groups was, in the words of Alain Destexhe, a former director of the medical humanitarian organization Doctors Without Borders, "not only a crime against the rules of war, but a crime against humanity itself." It affected not just a few individuals or even one or two countries, Destexhe says, but all of humanity. Moreover, he adds, the Nazis' crime was

> on a different scale to all other crimes against humanity. [It was] a conspiracy aimed at the total destruction of a group and thus required a concerted plan of action. The instigators and initiators [were] cool-minded theorists first and barbarians only second. The specificity of [the crime did] not arise from the extent of the killings, nor their savagery or resulting infamy, but solely from the intention: the destruction of a group.[2]

In 1944, a few months before World War II ended, Raphael Lemkin, a Polish-Jewish legal scholar who had managed to escape from the Nazis, was living in the United States. He coined a new word—*genocide*—to give this enormous crime against humanity a name at last. To create the new term, he combined the Greek word *genos*, meaning "race" or "tribe," with the Latin suffix *cide*, meaning "kill."

Trying to Define Genocide

When the war ended in 1945, the Allies sought to accurately and concisely define the "crimes against humanity" they felt the Nazis had committed. In Nuremberg, Germany, they prosecuted the surviving Nazi leaders as war criminals who carried out atrocities (unusually brutal acts) in what came to be called the Nuremberg trials. According to the "Charter of the International Military Tribunal" for the trial proceedings, the definition of crimes against humanity was determined as "murder, extermination, enslavement, deportation, and other inhumane acts committed against any civilian population, before or during the war; or persecutions on political, racial, or religious grounds . . . whether or not in violation of the domestic law of the country where perpetrated."[3]

The tribunal that ran the Nuremberg trials did not arrive at a precise definition for genocide, however. A definition came three years later, when the United Nations (UN), an international organization that was formed at the close of the war, adopted a new law called the Convention on the Prevention and Punishment of the Crime of Genocide. The vote to accept it was unanimous, and it went into force on January 12, 1951. In Article 2 of the convention genocide is defined as any of the following acts committed with intent to eliminate a national, ethnic, racial, or religious group, by

a. Killing members of the group;
b. Causing serious bodily or mental harm to members of the group;
c. Deliberately inflicting on the group conditions of life calculated to bring about its physical destruction in whole or in part;
d. Imposing measures intended to prevent births within the group;
e. Forcibly transferring children of the group to another group.[4]

Furthermore, hoping to prevent genocide from happening in the future, those who drafted the convention provided for punishing anyone who committed it. Article 4 states, "Persons committing genocide or any of the other acts enumerated in Article 3 shall be punished, whether they are constitutionally responsible rulers, public officials, or private individuals." Also, Article 6 says: "Persons charged with genocide or any of the other acts enumerated in Article 3 shall be tried by a competent tribunal of the State in the territory of which the act was committed, or by such international penal tribunal as may have jurisdiction [authority]."[5]

Ordinary People

Despite these efforts to define and prevent genocide, however, the gruesome

Nazi leaders sit in the dock at the Nuremberg trials in 1945. They were charged with "crimes against humanity," which included murder, extermination, enslavement, deportation, and inhumane acts against civilian populations.

phenomenon occurred again. Between 1975 and 1979, an estimated 1 to 3 million Cambodians, most of them belonging to ethnic minority groups, were murdered by death squads directed by the country's sadistic ruler, Pol Pot. Then came the Rwandan genocide in 1994. That makes at least four clear-cut cases of large-scale genocide that occurred in the twentieth century. (Along with the incidents in Germany, Cambodia, and Rwanda, most historians count the killing of some 1.2 million Armenians and Greeks by the Ottoman Turks between 1915 and 1920 as a case of genocide; however, the Turks vehemently deny the charge.)

Large numbers of people died in these well-known episodes of genocide. Yet it is not simply the number of people murdered that characterizes the phenomenon. Experts point out that most often genocide occurs when seemingly ordinary social groups and organizations that do not normally resort to violence suddenly do so, for reasons that vary. According to University of Wisconsin scholar Scott Straus, this involvement of otherwise everyday people in mass killings was a main feature of the Rwandan genocide. He writes,

Genocide is ultimately about how ordinary people come to see fellow citizens, neighbors, friends, loved ones, and even children as "enemies" who must be killed. Genocide is, moreover, a massively complex social phenomenon. Genocide involves a range of social institutions, from the state [government] to the military to the church, and the media. And in the Rwandan case, genocide included the participation of hundreds of thousands of individuals, of whom the majority had no prior history of committing lethal violence.[6]

This example of apparently ordinary citizens turning on and butchering their neighbors was a large part of what shocked the world in 1994. Of course, it also astonished many of the victims when people they had known for years, in some cases people they thought were friends, suddenly attacked them. Much of the horror of the incredible story of the Rwandan genocide can be summed up in the experience of twenty-two-year-old farmer Maranyunda Hill, whose father was one of the unfortunate victims. A while after the killings ended, she recalls:

Mama went to the trial of one of Papa's murderers, a neighbor. He encountered Mama in the hallway of the courthouse [and] said [good day] to her politely, asked about the family, the rains, our fields, [and then] said [good-bye] and returned to prison as if he were going home. Mama stood there with her mouth hanging open before she started to cry.[7]

Chapter One

Rwanda Before the Genocide

At first glance, visitors to pre-modern Rwanda could never have imagined that terrible mass murders would one day take place there. The first Europeans who entered the region in the 1890s found that it was a beautiful place with picturesque mountain ranges and pastures and an extremely pleasant climate. Also, its inhabitants seemed largely peaceful and productive. In 2010 Rwanda had nearly 11 million residents, making it the most densely populated nation in Africa. But in the nineteenth century it was far less crowded, with fewer than 2 million people. Moreover, in those days most Rwandans got along with one another, in stark contrast to the genocide that killed close to a million of the country's citizens in the 1990s.

A Highly Attractive Land

One feature that may have contributed to the tranquility of Rwanda in precolonial times (before it became a European colony in the late 1800s) was its magnificent physical setting. About the size of the U.S. state of Maryland, the country is situated in east-central Africa. Rwanda borders that continent's so-called Great Lakes region (which includes the huge lakes Victoria and Tanganyika) and lies south of the modern nation of Uganda and west of modern Tanzania. The early Rwandans came to call their home the "Land of a Thousand Hills" because of the numerous and attractive forest-covered peaks that dominate the region. Scattered between these rolling hills are pleasant green valleys with plenty of land suitable for farming.

Another inviting feature that drew people to the area and greatly contributed to their peace and prosperity was the local climate. Rwanda is located just north of the equator. Yet because most of its land is elevated well above sea level, it enjoys moderate rather than

Uganda

Kisoro ● Kabale

Zaire

Lac Burera

Ruhengeri ◉ Lac Ruhondo ◉ Byumba

Lac Rwanye

Lake Mujunju

Rwanda

Goma ● ◉ Gisenyi

Lac Kivu

Lac Muhazi

Lac Iherna

Kalehe ●

◈ Kigali

Nyabar Ongo

Kibuye ◉ Gitarama

Lac Mugesera

Lake Bisongou

Rwanda

Birurum

Mwogo

Bukavu ● ◉ Cyangugu

Nyanza ●

Gikongoro ◉

Butare ◉

Rweru

Cohoha

Kirundo ◉

Ruvuvu

Luhwa

Ruwa

Tanzania

Zaire

◉ Cibitoke

Ngozi ◉

Muyinga ◉

◉ Kayanza

Ruvubu

Mwrut

Bubanza ◉

Ulindi

Ruzizi

◉ Muramvya

◉ Karuzi

Ruvubu

◉ Cankuzo

Ruwiti

Uvira ●

◈ Bujumbura

◉ Gitega

◉ Ruyigi

Kibondo ●

Burundi

Lake Tanganyika

Bururi ◉

Rutana ◉

Rumonge ●

Murangasi

Fizi ●

◉ Makamba

Nyanza Lac ●

Tanzania

steaming hot temperatures for most of the year. According to Rwanda's ministry of education,

A combination of tropical location and high altitude ensures that most of Rwanda has a temperate year-round climate. Temperatures rarely stray above 30 degrees Celsius by day or below 15 degrees Celsius at night throughout the year. The exceptions are the chilly upper slopes of the Virunga Mountains, and the hot low-lying Tanzania border area protected in Akagera National Park. Throughout the country, seasonal variations in temperature are relatively insignificant. Most parts of the country receive in excess of 1,000mm of precipitation annually, with the driest months being July to September and the wettest February to May.[8]

Rwanda's Impressive Physical Setting

Spanning 10,169 square miles (26,338 sq. km), Rwanda is approximately the size of the U.S. state of Maryland and the Caribbean nation of Haiti. Rwanda is landlocked, as the country of Tanzania, to its east, lies between it and the Indian Ocean.

In addition to Tanzania, the countries bordering Rwanda include the Democratic Republic of Congo, in the west; Uganda, in the north; and Burundi, in the south. A hilly land, Rwanda features numerous small-to-moderate-size mountain chains. The tallest peaks are in the northwest, in the Virunga range, dominated by volcanoes, the largest being Mount Karisimbi, towering to 14,787 feet (4,507m). Most of the country's mountains and volcanoes are covered by verdant forests. The lowlands feature a diverse mix of picturesque pastures, rich farmlands, lovely river valleys, and swamps teeming with exotic plants and animals.

Mount Karisimbi, a dormant volcano that towers 14,787 feet, is Rwanda's tallest mountain.

Rwanda's highly agreeable climate and terrain also attracted numerous species of animals, which the early Rwandans came either to exploit for food or to coexist in harmony with. These creatures included cattle, which some Rwandans raised, and antelopes, zebras, and many species of birds, which other Rwandans hunted. Among the other plentiful animals inhabiting the region's lush forests, grasslands, and rivers were several species of monkeys and lemurs; large predators, including lions and wild dogs; hippos and elephants; and some of the last mountain gorillas left on the planet.

The Populating of Rwanda

Modern archaeologists and other experts are unsure of when the region now occupied by Rwanda was first inhabited. But there is a general consensus among them that primitive humans entered the area roughly ten thousand years ago. Evidence unearthed at various sites in Rwanda shows that these early residents were hunter-gatherers. They stalked, killed, and ate a wide range of local animals and collected and consumed various leaves, roots, berries, and herbs.

Eventually other groups of early Africans moved into and populated the region. At a date that remains uncertain, these included settlers who knew how to smelt metals from ores (rocks containing veins of metals) for making metal tools and weapons. They also possessed the skills to fashion simple pottery from clay. These were the ancestors of the Rwandan natives known as the Twa.

Later, beginning in about 700 B.C., people from the west, from what is now the Congo, arrived in Rwanda. An offshoot of a large group of peoples collectively called the Bantu, they called themselves Hutu. Effective farmers, they steadily came to outnumber the indigenous inhabitants and to push them away into the dense forests. A few centuries later, a third group entered the area from an African region that scholars have yet to identify. Calling themselves Tutsi, they sustained themselves mainly by raising cattle and other livestock.

Thus, by the time that Europe was in the midst of what historians call its early medieval era (ca. A.D. 500–1000), three groups of people, many of whom made their livings very much like medieval Europeans did, inhabited Rwanda. However, it would be misleading to see these early Rwandan groups as separate and highly culturally distinct as they became in early modern times. Indeed, the native Rwandans did not belong to separate races, and they seem to have viewed themselves as more or less culturally unified. French scholar Louis de Lacger, who wrote a classic history of Rwanda in the 1950s, remarked,

One of the most surprising phenomena of Rwanda's [early] human geography is surely the contrast between the plurality of [local groups] and the sentiment of national unity. The natives of this country genuinely have the feeling of forming but one people. [They] were persuaded before the European penetration [of the region] that their country was the center of the world, that this was the largest, most powerful, and most civilized kingdom on earth, [and] they found it natural that the two horns of the crescent moon should be turned toward Rwanda [seeming to single it out among all other places and peoples].[9]

The Kingdom of Rwanda

Lacger's use of the term *civilized kingdom* refers to the first major, successful nation-state in the region—the Kingdom of Rwanda. It was established some time in the 1300s or 1400s along the shores of Lake Muhazi, a long, narrow waterway lying in the area's eastern sector. At first the kingdom competed with other regional powers lying to its west.

Tutsi warriors pose for the camera. Descendents of people collectively called the Bantu and the Hutu settled in Rwanda around 700 B.C.

Rwanda's Mountain Gorillas

This brief summary of Rwanda's gorillas, of which about 355 still survived in 2010, is from a 2002 article in the Chicago Tribune *newspaper.*

Today, 354 of the world's most endangered gorillas slip through the misty rainforest below Rwanda's towering Virunga volcanoes. . . . [Overall] about 654 of the woolly black gorillas, first described by a German explorer a century ago and made famous by . . . American [scientist] Dian Fossey, survive in two small areas of cool mountain forest in Uganda and on the Rwanda-Congo border. On a continent where great apes are disappearing with dismaying speed to hunting and habitat loss, they are the rarest cousins in the [primate] family. . . . Foreign visits to the gorillas dropped to zero in 1994, when genocide swept across the nation [but] tourism is now rebuilding, and with hundreds of foreign visitors a month handing over $250 each to [be led into the forest by park rangers to] see the gorillas, the government has a powerful new incentive to protect them.

Laurie Goering, "Gorillas Beat Odds Amid War in Rwanda," *Chicago Tribune*, August 12, 2002. http://articles .chicagotribune.com/2002-08-12/news/0208120174_1_international-gorilla-conservation-program-mountain-gorillas-rwanda.

Rwanda is the last refuge of the mountain gorillas. They are the world's most endangered gorillas.

But it steadily absorbed them, becoming larger and more powerful and eventually occupied all the land from Lake Muhazi to the much larger Lake Kivu (on the border of what is now Congo).

Later, in the late 1500s or early 1600s, the Rwandan kingdom was invaded by the Banyoro, another Bantu group that lived in what is now Uganda. The reigning Rwandan *Unwami* (or *Mwami*), the local word for "king," had no choice but to flee and set up a new residence somewhere to the west. However, later in the 1600s a strong Rwandan *Unwami*, Ruganzu Ndori, and his successors managed to retake their homeland and the Kingdom of Rwanda became more powerful than ever.

Ndori and other premodern Rwandan kings took the throne by inheriting it from a relative or other member of their clan. In that era the dominant clan, which supplied the majority of the kings, was the Nyiginya clan, a Tutsi group. The king possessed a great deal of authority. But he was not an absolute monarch because he shared power to some degree with other high authority figures. As researchers Philip Briggs and Janice Booth explain:

> The centralized control by the king was blocked by a very powerful queen mother and a group [called] the *abiiru*. [The] *abiiru* could reverse the king's decisions if they conflicted with the magical [moral code] protected and interpreted by the *abiiru*. They also governed the selection of a new king. Any member of the *abiiru* who forgot any part of

his assigned portion of the [moral code] was punished severely.[10]

Beneath the royal family and other authority figures in the Rwandan kingdom's hierarchy, or political and social ladder, were a few wealthy cattle owners and planters somewhat equivalent to the landed nobles of medieval and early modern Europe. These Rwandan overlords were viewed as socially superior to the ordinary peasants who made up the bulk of the population. The lords and peasants had a working relationship known as *ubuhake*. Similar in some ways to the patronage system that developed in ancient Rome, *ubuhake* was in essence an economic arrangement in which the peasants worked and did favors for a handful of rich patrons, or lords. In return the lords provided protection to and occasionally did favors for their underprivileged peasants.

The complex relationships among Rwandans of various classes revolved almost exclusively around the chief economic methods employed in the kingdom. As they had been for many centuries, these were cattle raising (pastoralism) and farming (agriculture, or cultivation). Therefore, almost all Rwandans were either pastoralists or cultivators, and the king and other government officials developed close working relationships with both groups. According to the human rights organization, Human Rights Watch,

> Although the power of the ruler derived from control over the

military and over cattle, his authority was buttressed also by rituals firmly rooted in agricultural practices. By the end of the nineteenth century [the 1800s], the ruler governed the central regions closely through multiple hierarchies of competing officials who administered men, cattle, pasturage [grazing lands], and agricultural land. He exercised a looser kind of [control] over other areas, particularly on the [outer edges of the kingdom], which were dominated by powerful lineage groups, some of them pastoralists, some cultivators. In addition, he tolerated the existence of several small [chiefdoms] within the boundaries of Rwanda, usually because their rulers were thought to control rainfall, crop pests, or some other aspect of agricultural productivity important for Rwanda as a whole.[11]

Much like today the early Rwandans raised cattle and farmed the land. Cattle represented wealth in the society.

Enter the Germans

Unfortunately for the Rwandans, their agricultural and other productivity did not always remain theirs alone to exploit. Like many other African kingdoms and territories, in the late 1800s Rwanda became a target of wholesale colonization by the leading European powers. Europe had long exploited Africa's coasts for various trade goods, including slaves. But Europeans knew very little about the continent's interior regions until the mid- to late nineteenth century. They increasingly saw Africa's abundant raw materials and agricultural lands as ripe for the taking. Furthermore, they realized they could exploit African workers because they could pay them far less than their European counterparts.

These motives, along with the desire to convert Africans to Christianity, drove what became known as Europe's "scramble for Africa" in the late 1800s and early 1900s. Belgium's king Leopold II realized that the European powers might well come to blows over who would seize which African kingdom. Hoping to avoid such conflicts, he convinced Germany's leader, Otto von Bismarck, to convene a large meeting of these powers in Berlin, Germany, late in 1884. Delegates from Germany, France, Britain, Austria-Hungary, Belgium, Russia, Spain, Turkey, and other major nations drew up an agreement in which most of Africa was partitioned, or divided up, into European colonies. The Africans themselves, whom the Europeans viewed as inferiors, had no say in deciding their own destinies.

During the conference in Berlin, what is now Rwanda, then called Ruanda-Urundi, came under Germany's control. Together with neighboring Tanganyika, Rwanda became part of the new colony of German East Africa. Incredibly, none of the Germans who took charge of Rwanda had ever visited that land or talked to its residents. In fact, at that time the Germans and other Europeans had no clear idea of how big Rwanda was or what it even looked like. The rule of thumb for the great powers was that if one could gain control of a coastal sector of Africa, one was entitled to seize the territories stretching inland from that coast for hundreds of miles. Britain's Lord Salisbury famously summed up this strange and lopsided policy, saying, "We [Europeans] have been giving away mountains and rivers and lakes to each other, only hindered by the small impediment [obstacle] that we never knew exactly where they were."[12]

Intending to remedy this situation and find out more about its new Rwandan possession, the German government sent explorer Gustav Adolf von Götzen to inspect and map the region in 1894. He was only the second European ever to set foot in Rwanda. (The first had been an Austrian mapmaker, Oscar Baumann.) Götzen traveled around the country, reacting with amazement when he saw the enormous Lake Kivu and having long meetings with the reigning Rwandan king. In the years that followed, other Germans arrived, among them some military personnel and Christian missionaries. But

At the instigation of King Leopold II of Belgium, European powers met for the Berlin Conference to carve up central Africa for the Europeans in 1884.

the most important newcomers were so-called advisers, who were assigned to the king and his leading chiefs. The advisers claimed that they were there to help the Rwandans prosper and learn to deal with the wider world that they knew little about. The Germans also left the country's existing social structure and divisions more or less in place. In that way they hoped to keep the allegiance of the ruling class, which naturally desired to perpetuate its control over the peasants. Because most of the native rulers were Tutsis, the Germans themselves soon came to assume that the Tutsis were somehow superior to other groups in the kingdom.

Thus, the Germans somewhat discreetly ruled Rwanda by advising and thereby loosely controlling its rulers. Their advice always favored Germany's interests in the region, of course. But for the most part the country's political and social institutions remained intact. This was because Germany was not yet ready to invest the money and manpower necessary to significantly overhaul the country.

New, Harsher Colonizers

The Germans might well have gone on to transform Rwanda if they had not gotten involved in World War I (1914–1918). During that immense conflict, Germany,

Austria-Hungary, and the Turkish Ottoman Empire squared off against the Allies, which included France, Britain, Belgium, the United States, and other major powers. Midway through the war, in 1916, Belgium wrestled control of Ruanda-Urundi from Germany. Then, in 1919, with the great conflict over, the future Rwanda came under the wing of the League of Nations, a new international organization dedicated to maintaining world peace. The league authorized Belgium to continue governing the Rwandans.

Unlike the Germans, who kept most local institutions and customs intact, the Belgians made numerous changes. They imposed European-style practices in public works, education, health facilities, and agriculture. The Belgians introduced new methods in agriculture that helped to reduce famines that periodically struck the country, and they pushed hard for the Rwandans to make a large profit from farming. To this end, Belgian officials insisted that coffee become a major cash crop and expected every local farmer to set aside part of his land for raising coffee beans. Over time many Rwandans were subjected to harsh forced labor. Those who disobeyed were whipped, which induced thousands of

"A Place in the Sun"

The European colonization of African kingdoms and territories, including Rwanda, in the 1800s and 1900s was swift and decisive. It was also done in an arrogant, selfish manner, with no thought to Rwandan sovereignty or needs. After seizing control of Rwanda and other African lands, German leader Kaiser Wilhelm II said,

We have conquered for ourselves a place in the sun. It will now be my task to see to it that this place in the sun shall remain our undisputed possession, in order that the sun's rays may fall fruitfully upon our activity and trade in foreign parts, that our industry and agriculture may develop within the state and our sailing sports upon the water. . . . When the German has once learned to direct his glance upon what is distant and great, the pettiness which surrounds him in daily life on all sides will disappear. As head of the Empire I therefore rejoice over every citizen . . . who goes forth with this large outlook and seeks new points where we can drive in the nail on which to hang our armor.

Quoted in Christian F. Gauss, *The German Kaiser as Shown in His Public Utterances*. New York: Scribner, 1915, pp. 181–183.

farmers to flee to neighboring Uganda.

The Belgians also played local groups against one another in an attempt to keep all Rwandans unstable, weak, and less likely to try to rebel. One prominent, educated Rwandan who survived the genocide in the 1990s recalls:

The new colonizers looked at the social rift [separation] between our leaders and farmers and saw an easy way to rule. . . . It was a version of the old divide-and-conquer tactics used so effectively by colonizers throughout history, [including] separating the haves from the have-nots.[13]

In addition, the Belgians sometimes exerted direct control over and/or manipulated the Rwandan kings. This was especially true for the rulers who became fed up with the outsiders' colonial policies. In 1931, for instance, *Unwami* Yuhi IV decided to try to drive away the Belgians and plotted against them. So they removed him from power and replaced him with a Tutsi puppet ruler, *Unwami* Mutara III, who largely did their bidding.

The Coming of Independence

Belgium's handling of Rwanda, then still called Ruanda-Urundi, and its people began to change at the close of World War II in 1945. The League of Nations was dissolved to make way for the United Nations (UN), a new and larger international organization. Rwanda's surviv-al and welfare became the responsibility of the UN, which allowed Belgium to continue administering the country. However, the Belgians now found themselves under closer scrutiny than they were used to by UN officials and other nations. Also, members of a powerful new worldwide movement, often called Pan-Africanism, began to demand that Europe's African colonies be allowed to work toward their independence.

Responding to these developments, new movements arose within Rwanda as well. Nearly all Rwandans wanted independence, but there were differing views about how it should come about. Some wanted the existing system, a monarchy largely controlled by socially dominant Tutsis, to continue after the country had gained self-rule. An opposing group, known as the Hutu emancipation movement, headed by Grégoire Kayibanda, a prominent Hutu, lobbied for a more even-handed system. Of course Kayibanda was well aware that because the Hutus greatly outnumbered the Tutsis, the Hutus would likely dominate the new government he envisioned. As for the Belgians, for various political reasons they abruptly switched their longtime support from the monarchy to the Hutu emancipation movement.

Because of the sharp disagreements about how to proceed toward independence, outbreaks of violence erupted between rival groups in November 1959. Several thousand people were killed and thousands more were intimidated into moving to neighboring countries. Not long afterward, the Belgian authorities

Belgium granted independence to Rwanda in 1962. Gregiore Kayibanda was elected Rwanda's first prime minister.

oversaw democratic elections that got rid of the ancient monarchy and created the beginnings of a republic. Between 1960 and 1961, Ruanda-Urundi was divided into two separate states—Rwanda and Burundi. The following year the Belgians granted full independence to both, and Kayibanda became Rwanda's first prime minister. Soon afterward he was elected president. One Rwandan remembers the official handover of power that transformed Rwanda from a European colony into a new, independent nation. He says:

Belgium and the United Nations handed the nation over to a Hutu government and left the nation after a brief ceremony on July 1, 1962, at 10 o'clock in the morning. A new flag was hastily designed and raised: a tricolor banner with a plain letter R in the middle. These events, taken as a whole, [placed the Hutu in power in Rwanda].[14]

In the years that followed, Kayibanda's government became increasingly unpopular in Rwanda. This was mainly because he and his followers refused to share power with other groups. This unstable situation paved the way for a largely bloodless coup (government takeover) led by prominent army officer Juvénal Habyarimana in 1973.

As the country's new president, Habyarimana promised to bring about increased prosperity, which for a while he did. He also said that he would work toward bringing all national groups together. But over time it became evident that this was not happening fast enough or on a large enough scale. Distrust and dislike between rival factions in Rwanda continued, as did discrimination against some, particularly Tutsi. In addition, Habyarimana, like Kayibanda before him, increasingly consolidated his own power, acting more like a dictator than a democratic president. These developments led to mounting tensions in Rwanda that no one then realized were destined eventually to erupt into mass murder on an enormous scale.

Chapter Two

The Roots of Hatred

In the years following the Rwandan genocide, people around the world were shocked by the brutal event and asked what had caused it. Many outside observers, particularly in Western countries like Britain and the United States, thought the main reason for the violence was tribal warfare or tribalism. But scholars and other observers who are familiar with Rwanda's history say that this is woefully misleading. It is true, they admit, that some parts of Africa were and still are largely tribal. That is, their local populations consist of separate clans and other groups that have distinct differences, often including dissimilar social customs and languages. However, as political scientist Scott Straus points out:

Tribe is the wrong [term] for describing Rwanda's ethnic categories. Rwanda has three commonly recognized ethnic groups—Hutus, Tutsis, and Twas. [In whatever ways] scholars understand the categories' origins, the groups are most certainly not "tribal." Hutus and Tutsis speak the same language (Kinyarwanda); they belong to the same clans; they live in the same regions . . . they have the same cultural practices [and] they have the same religions. Many also intermarry.[15]

Paul Rusesabagina, the hotel manager whose saving of many lives during the massacres was dramatized in the film *Hotel Rwanda*, agrees. He makes the point that many people in the West mistakenly assume that all tribal peoples were and remain primitive and/or backward and says,

It always bothers me when I hear Rwanda's genocide described as the product of "ancient tribal hatreds." I think this is an easy way for Westerners to dismiss the whole thing as a regrettable but pointless bloodbath that happens to primitive brown people. . . . Nothing could be further from the truth. [The genocide] may have been accomplished with crude agricultural tools instead of gas chambers, but [the victims] were killed [with] a calculated efficiency that would have impressed the most rigorous accountant.[16]

Thus, the vast majority of Rwandans were similar to one another rather than culturally different. This fact naturally raises the question of why the country's national groups came to hate one another so much. A major part of the answer emerges when one examines in more detail the manner in which European colonizers played one Rwandan group against another. Indeed, it was mainly in the nation's colonial period that the deep hatreds that eventually ignited the genocide took root.

Traditional Social Differences

One important aspect of the long-standing relationship and interactions between Rwanda's rival groups is demography, or the breakdown and dynamics of the population. As is true in many other countries, the majority of the inhabitants make up one group, and minorities constitute the other groups. In the late twentieth century, shortly before the genocide, the Hutus made up about 84 to 90 percent of the population; Tutsis represented roughly 9 to 15 percent; and about 1 percent were Twas. The population breakdown shortly before and during the colonial period is not very well known. But most scholars think it was similar to that of the late twentieth century. That is, the Hutus made up the bulk of the population, and Tutsis were considerably less numerous.

This population breakdown was misleading in an important way. At first glance one might assume that the Hutus, who were numerically dominant, would also dominate the political and social scenes. However, exactly the opposite was true. It has been established that the monarchy was most often controlled by one or another of the leading Tutsi clans. In fact, most of the early kings and nobles were Tutsis, and a majority of the peasants were Hutus and Twas. This reality is reflected in the origins of the names of these groups. It is also evident in the way said names came to describe the country's social roles and stereotypes. Human Rights Watch, a human rights organization, explains:

As the Rwandan [kingdom] grew in strength and sophistication, the governing elite became more clearly defined and its members, like powerful people in most societies, began to think of themselves as superior to ordinary people. The word "Tutsi," which apparently first described the status of an individual—a person rich in cattle—became the term that referred to the elite group as a whole

A Tutsi tribesman (background) guards Hutu captives. From colonial times the minority Tutsi clans controlled the majority Hutus and Twas.

and the word "Hutu"—meaning originally a subordinate or follower of a more powerful person—came to refer to the mass of the ordinary people. . . . The Twas, a people clearly differentiated from Hutus and Tutsis, formed the smallest component of the Rwandan population. . . . Originally forest dwellers who lived by hunting and gathering, [the] Twas [were most often] potters, laborers, or servants. [They] also used to speak a distinctive form of Kinyarwanda.[17]

Fortunately for the precolonial Rwandans, these social differences between the various local groups, which were basically economic and class distinctions, were seen as fairly minor difficulties. Intermarriages among members of the groups, especially between Hutus and Tutsis, were reasonably common, and violence among the groups was rare.

A New Racial Divide

When the European colonizers seized control of Rwanda, however, this traditional, largely peaceful state of affairs began to change and was eventually distorted beyond recognition. In particular the Belgians turned what had long been primarily economic and class differences into supposedly racial and ethnic ones. There was ample precedent for

The White Man in the Bushes

In the late twentieth century Rwanda was unusually crowded for an African nation, as made clear in the following humorous anecdote told by a Western doctor who worked in Rwanda in the late 1980s.

One day as [my colleague] and I were driving to a remote health center in the north of the country, we stopped by the roadside so that I could urinate. I walked well into what I thought was secluded bush [woods]. While I peed, I became aware that I was being watched. Many children had gathered . . . apparently from nowhere. They stared and smiled at the white man peeing in the bushes. Coming from the vastness of Canada, it was a strange feeling for me, that even in the bush I could not be alone.

James Orbinski, *An Imperfect Offering: Humanitarian Action for the Twenty-First Century*. New York: Walker, 2008, p. 44.

this attempt to manipulate the native population. After establishing a new colony, European colonial administrators frequently selected a local group of individuals, usually members of a privileged social class, to aid them and act as intermediaries with the general native masses.

For this task the Belgians chose the less-numerous Tutsis, who had a history of economic and political privilege. But as Straus explains, the colonial authorities sought to further increase the gap of superiority between this subclass and other Rwandans by introducing divisive racial overtones:

In the Rwandan Tutsis, the European explorers and missionaries believed that they had found a "superior" "race" of "natural-born rulers." Europeans wrote that Tutsis had migrated with their cattle from northern Africa at some earlier time and had come to dominate the more lowly Hutus, which Europeans considered an inferior "race" of Bantu "negroids." This reflected the [scientific] ideas of the day . . . which saw civilization in Africa as the product of "Caucasoid" [white, or light-skinned] peoples. However strange such a way of seeing the world strikes the contemporary reader, the colonial period was rife [filled] with such theories. Colonial-era documents consistently describe Hutus as short, stocky, dark-skinned, and wide-nosed. By contrast, the Tutsis are presented as tall, elegant, light-skinned, and thin-nosed. [In line with these ideas] Belgian colonial officials [eventually] introduced identity cards that labeled Rwandans according to their ethnicity.[18]

Working in tandem with the Belgians in separating the Hutus and Tutsis into distinct groups was the Catholic Church. Catholic missionaries ardently promoted the so-called Hamitic theory, which suggested that the Tutsis originally came from a "superior," white, Christian race. Unfortunately for the Rwandans, this hypothesis was completely fabricated and constituted only part of the priests' manipulation of the local population. According to a postgenocide report by the Organization of African Union,

It is not possible to write about Rwanda without writing about the role of the Catholic Church. [Much] of the elaborate [Hamitic myth] was simply invented by the Catholic White Fathers, missionaries who wrote what later became the established version of Rwandan history to conform to their essentially racist views. Because they controlled all schooling in the colony, the White Fathers were able, with the full endorsement of the Belgians, to indoctrinate generations of school children, both Hutu and Tutsi, with the pernicious [harmful] Hamitic notions. . . . Together, the Belgians and the Catholic Church were guilty of what some call "eth-

nogenesis," the [establishment] of rigid ethnic identities for political purposes . . . to politicize and polarize society through ethnic cleavages [separation].[19]

Working together, the Belgian and Catholic authorities steadily exaggerated, fabricated, and/or reinforced the social differences between the Tutsis and Hutus. In the 1920s and 1930s under the Belgian colonial system, only Tutsis were allowed to become government officials. Hutus were not only barred from holding influential positions, but they were also discriminated against in education, hiring, and other areas. One exception to this rule was that some Hutus were allowed to study in religious seminaries.

The Belgians and church fathers were eminently satisfied with the resulting racially divided society. This was because it mirrored the similar discriminatory social systems that then existed in most parts of Europe, as well as in the United States, systems widely viewed by whites as natural and ordained by God. According to Human Rights Watch, those who perpetuated these systems

believed [that] Tutsis, Hutus, and Twas were three distinct, long-existent and internally coherent blocks of people. Unclear whether these were races, tribes, or language groups, the Europeans were nonetheless certain that the Tutsis were superior to the Hutus and the Hutus superior to the Twas—just as they knew themselves to be superior to all three. . . . Believing the Tutsis to be more capable, they found it logical for the Tutsis to rule [the] Hutus and Twas just as it was reasonable for Europeans to rule Africans. Not surprisingly, [many] Tutsis welcomed these ideas about their superiority [and] they supplied data to the European clergy and academics who produced the first written histories of Rwanda. The collaboration resulted in a sophisticated and convincing but inaccurate history that simultaneously served Tutsi interests and validated European assumptions. [By] assuring a Tutsi monopoly of power, the Belgians set the stage for future conflict in Rwanda.[20]

Thus, the roots of hatred in modern Rwandan society were for the most part not planted by the natives themselves, but rather by the European intruders. In particular the Belgians were to blame for introducing racial differences into the societal mix. Under colonialism, Straus writes,

Race overshadowed the organization of society, [and] race became the country's central political idiom [theme]. The "ancient tribal hatred" model of the genocide misses this history. To claim that Hutus and Tutsis have hated each other for centuries and that this age-old hatred fueled the genocide are gross oversimplifications.[21]

The Belgians worked with the Catholic Church to reinforce and exploit the social differences between the Tutsis and the Hutus that sowed the seeds of future hatred between the tribes.

The Hutu Revolution

Although the Belgian authorities had long helped the Tutsis maintain control of the government and to discriminate against Hutus, various events eventually caused them to change these practices. One of the more important events occurred in November 1959. Several Tutsis beat up a local Hutu chief, and as word of the assault spread, Hutus attacked Tutsis in many parts of the country. Several hundred people were killed before Belgian officials restored order.

Hoping to stave off further violence and discord, these officials replaced about half of the Tutsis in the government with Hutus. Then came the abolishment of the Tutsi-dominated monarchy in 1961 and the establishment of Grégoire Kayibanda's Hutu-dominated government in 1962. Together these events became known as the Hutu Revolution.

After being held down for so long, Hutu officials took full advantage of their newfound political gains. They came to equate their enhanced political and social status with the concept of democracy. Furthermore in the name of democracy and what they viewed as justice, some Hutus intermittently attacked or drove away Tutsis in the early 1960s. The Human Rights Watch states:

> At the start, Hutus attacked powerholders and those related to them, leaving their ordinary Tutsi neighbors in peace. They usually sought to drive Tutsis away rather than to destroy them. [Many] displaced Tutsis resettled elsewhere in Rwanda [but] another 10,000 took the road to exile. [Some] of these refugees [soon] began to attack Rwanda, [and] after these incursions Hutu officials led reprisal attacks on Tutsis still within the country, accusing them of having aided the invaders. . . . Hutu leaders used [this violence] to bolster the sense of Hutu solidarity, to solidify their own control, [and] from these attacks they crafted the myth of the Hutu Revolution as a long and courageous struggle against ruthless forces of repression. [They came to use] the ideas once prized by the Tutsis—ideas about Tutsi distinctiveness, foreign origins, and complete control over the Hutus—to justify the violence of the revolution and the discriminatory measures of the years after.[22]

Single-Party Government

Once the Hutus were in power, anti-Tutsi feelings and acts became increasingly commonplace. During the 1960s, Hutu officials, led by President Kayibanda, established what was in effect a single-party government that did nothing to discourage discrimination against Tutsis. This attitude encouraged scattered attacks on Tutsi that broke out in 1973. Some Hutus blamed other Hutus for these assaults, so tensions swiftly rose between Hutus as well as between Hutus and Tutsis. Claiming to want to

After Juvénal Habyarimana seized power from Kayibanda he divided Rwanda into ten prefectures and appointed tribal leaders.

restore order, in July of that year Juvénal Habyarimana stepped out of the ranks of the army officer corps and seized power. Two years later he made the unofficial single-party government official, calling the party the National Revolutionary Movement for Development. Already the president, Habyarimana now became the head of the party as well.

To ensure that the government maintained control of all parts of the country, Habyarimana took advantage of and streamlined the existing organization of administrative units and citizens. Rwanda was divided into ten statelike prefectures. Each prefecture was composed of several smaller units called communes (of which 145 existed in 1991). Each commune had between thirty thousand and one hundred thousand people. The leader of a commune was called a burgomaster. He held meetings one or more times a week to give advice, settle local disputes, and so forth. (Habyarimana came to know all the burgomasters well and could hire and fire them at will.) Each Rwandan commune further broke down into subunits called sectors and cells, each with one or more local leaders who reported back to the burgomaster.

This overall administrative breakdown made it easy for the president to control all parts of the country. Whenever he gave an order, it quickly passed down through the ranks and was forced on the people at all levels. Moreover, later, during the genocide, this chain of command would prove brutally efficient. Habyarimana also headed the army, which featured some seven thousand soldiers, including between one thousand and thirteen hundred men who guarded the president. Thus, although Rwanda was technically a republic, it was actually a dictatorship. People who openly criticized the president could lose their jobs or worse. In addition the local Catholic Church supported Habyarimana enthusiastically. Among other favors, clergymen often made government announcements for him from the pulpit.

The Civil War

For a number of years Habyarimana did not discriminate against the Tutsis as much as his predecessor, Kayibanda, had. But the new president certainly did not go out of his way to encourage equality between Hutus and Tutsis. This was demonstrated in an incident that occurred in 1974. Many Hutus loudly complained that too many Tutsis were becoming doctors, teachers, and other professionals. As a result of these protests, local leaders forced thousands of Tutsis to resign from their jobs, and Habyarimana allowed it to happen.

Nevertheless, over time the president began to respond to calls, from both inside and outside of the country, for Rwanda to return to a fairer system of multiparty rule. In July 1990 he announced that he would work toward that goal. By that time, however, it was too late for the regime to avoid the anger of those Tutsis who had chosen to use violence to overthrow the country's repressive government. Beginning in the early 1960s, groups of Tutsis had gone into exile in Uganda and other neighboring countries. By 1990 they numbered an estimated six hundred thousand. Even more significantly, in 1987 the more militant among these refugees founded the Rwandan Patriotic Front (RPF). Its goal was to invade Rwanda, get rid of Habyarimana, and establish a real democracy.

The RPF's invasion, which initiated a Rwandan civil war, began on October 1, 1990. By October 4, the rebels had reached a point only 45 miles (72km) from the capital, Kigali. Then Habyarimana resorted to telling a big and daring lie. He claimed that RPF soldiers had entered Kigali and begun murdering people. Nearly all Rwandans believed this lie, and it allowed the president to rally considerable support against the RPF. It also allowed him to accuse the resident Tutsis of being the invaders' accomplices, which was only rarely the case. As a result, many people, most of them Tutsis, were arrested and held without charge. Most foreign governments also believed Habyarimana's lie, and Belgium and France sent troops to help him keep the rebels at bay.

Agreement at Arusha

For a while it looked as though Habyarimana would prevail and that single-party rule and anti-Tutsi discrimination would continue. How-

Rwandan Patriotic Front Tutsi rebels invaded Rwanda in October 1990 with the aim of deposing Habyarimana and establishing a democracy.

The Arusha Accords

The Arusha Accords emerged from a series of long, difficult negotiations between Juvénal Habyarimana's government and the Rwandan Patriotic Front (RPF) in Arusha, Tanzania. The agreement was designed to reduce tensions and violence in Rwanda, while promoting a constructive new national structure that would benefit and treat fairly all Rwandans, regardless of supposed ethnic differences. The complex document was shaped in numerous ways by Tanzania's well-meaning president, Ali Hassan Mwinyi. He not only mediated the lengthy talks, but also made helpful suggestions for ways that the opposing Rwandan parties might share power in a coalition government. Other crucial issues debated at Arusha included what to do about the thousands of refugees who had fled Rwanda in recent years; how to move, in careful stages, toward eventual free elections; and how to rebuild the country's economy, which had been badly damaged by years of bitter political disputes and civil strife. The Arusha Accords also called for a neutral international force of peacekeepers to oversee the agreement's implementation.

ever, the same foreign nations that had felt the need to prop him up, especially France, now strongly pressured him to recognize other political parties besides his own. Fearing that his power was eroding, Habyarimana gave in and in April 1992 formed a coalition government with an opposition party made up of moderate Hutus. Other, smaller political parties formed at the same time but had no direct say in the government.

As pressure from France, the United States, the UN, and other outsiders grew, the new government opened peace talks with the RPF. These talks

committed Habyarimana to a number of reforms, including the establishment of the rule of law, political power-sharing, the repatriation [return] and resettlement of refugees, and the integration of the armed forces to include the RPF. . . . The agreement was signed in August 1993 and [meant to be] implemented within 37 days, overseen by the United Nations.[23]

Because the agreement was signed in Arusha, it became known as the Arusha Accords. To further ensure that the accords would work, the UN sent troops to Rwanda in October 1993. Called the United Nations Assistance Mission for Rwanda (UNAMIR), it was commanded by General Romeo Dallaire, a Canadian military officer. The soldiers came from

Opposition to the Arusha Accords

After the Arusha Accords were agreed on by Juvénal Habyarimana's government and the Rwandan Patriotic Front (RPF), radical hard-liners in Rwanda's government wasted no time in plotting ways to undermine them. A mere two days after the signing of the agreement, Belgian military officials heard rumors that the hard-liners might try to foment public demonstrations and maybe even assassinations in an effort to scuttle the formation of a new, more democratic government. Some of the hard-liners were military officers who believed that their army could still defeat the RPF rebels if given enough time. They also believed that if the accords were implemented, many of those same officers might be demobilized and lose their jobs and salaries. Théoneste Bagosora was particularly opposed to the accords for this reason. A number of burgomasters (leaders of communes) and other local Rwandan officials also feared losing their positions and/or influence over the people. In addition, all of the hard-liners and their supporters worried that the new government would be dominated by Tutsis, who would trample on Hutu rights. For these and similar reasons, the hard-liners stepped up anti-Tutsi propaganda and began planning possible violent acts against Tutsis across the country.

Colonel Théoneste Bagorosa was opposed to the accords because he feared he would lose his job and salary. Many government military officers felt the same way.

several nations, among them Tunisia, Canada, and Belgium.

Despite the presence of these troops, and unfortunately for all involved, the accords were never fully implemented. This was partly because at about the same time that the troops arrived in Rwanda, civil strife erupted in neighboring Burundi. Soldiers and refugees spilling over the border into Rwanda further inflamed the tensions that already existed among the rival Rwandan groups. Also, the hard-liners among the Hutus, including several of the president's chief advisers and supporters, did not intend to give up power without a fight, in spite of the accords. Over the years, the roots of hatred had grown and matured, and an ominous affliction borne of that hatred—known as "Hutu Power"—was about to rear its hideous head and help to send Rwanda down a terrible path.

Chapter Three

Power, Planning, and Propaganda

All of the historians and other experts who have studied the Rwandan genocide agree that it was not a sudden, accidental, or spontaneous event. Nor was it an impulsive, unprompted tribal or ethnic clash. Rather, the reasons for it were complicated and the immediate lead up to the mass killings was coldly calculated and purposely planned. One foreign war correspondent who is familiar with the country's history explains it this way:

> Scratch below the surface of this genocide and you will find not a simple issue of tribal hatreds but a complex web of politics, economics, history, psychology, and a struggle for identity. What happened in Rwanda was the result of cynical manipulation by powerful political and military leaders. Faced with the choice of sharing their power with the Rwandan Patriotic Front [RPF],

they chose to vilify the RPF's main support group, the Tutsis. The authorities told the Hutus that the Tutsis planned to take their land. They summoned up memories of the colonial days when the Tutsi overlordship had guaranteed second-class citizenship for the Hutus. [The authorities said] "Remember your shame. Remember how they humiliated us. Be proud of your Hutu blood."[24]

By the early 1990s the "powerful political and military leaders" mentioned above had already managed to create the first of three conditions required for genocide to occur. Namely, they had acquired a great deal of power over the populace. The other two conditions are planning and propaganda. The killings were well thought out and in many cases carefully planned ahead of time. Also, the hard-liners who did this planning skillfully employed propaganda in the form of lies and appeals to fear in an effort to whip up Hutus across Rwanda into a frenzy. These efforts were appallingly effective. Often, people who had never before thought themselves capable of committing murder became convinced that it was necessary to do so. One Rwandan later told an American journalist a fact that lay at the very heart of the genocide and indeed made it possible. "People are not inherently bad," he said. "But they can be made bad."[25]

Hutu Power

Probably the single most effective tool utilized by the potent forces of power, planning, and propaganda on the eve of the genocide was the menacing movement, or philosophy, known as Hutu Power. The Hutu hard-liners in national, regional, and local government hated the Tutsis and the RPF with a passion and refused to consider sharing power with them. Also, they were disgusted with the Arusha Accords and disappointed with President Habyarimana. They viewed his willingness to negotiate with the RPF as a serious weakness. During the talks in Arusha, radical Hutus frequently claimed that the Tutsis were manipulating Habyarimana.

In addition, the hard-liners said, the country's prime minister, Agathe Uwilingiyimana, a so-called Tutsi lover, was poisoning the president's mind. Rwanda's first and only female prime minister, Uwilingiyimana, a Hutu, was then forty. A former chemist and teacher, she believed in fair treatment of Tutsis and

supported the Arusha Accords. These moderate stances naturally angered the hard-liners, who saw her as a traitor.

In 1993 after the signing of the Arusha Accords, the hard-liners began forming their own, even more extreme offshoot of the existing, already radical Hutu governing party. The new movement received its name from the speeches of the highly placed and popular Hutu politician Froduald

Froduald Karamira led the hard-line Hutu opposition to the Arusha Accords and called on fellow Hutus to unite against the Tutsis.

Karamira. He drew widespread support in mass rallies, including one in late October 1993. During his speech, Karamira called for all Rwandan Hutus to unite against the Tutsis, both outside and inside the country. The leaders of the RPF had "lied to us in Arusha when they were signing for peace and democracy!" he shouted.

> We are not simply "heating heads" by saying we have plans "to work." [We all must help the government] look for what is within us. The enemy [is] among us here. We cannot sit down and think that [nothing is amiss]. We have clarified what we must avoid. [We must] avoid fighting another Hutu. We have been attacked, so let us not attack ourselves. Let us avoid the invasion of the enemy who may steal our government.[26]

The crowd then answered Karamira with a continuous roar of "Pawa! Pawa! Pawa!"[27] (*Pawa* is the Kinyarwanda equivalent of the English word *power*). Consequently, the movement, as well as its aims and philosophy, soon came to known as Hutu Power.

Those who advocated Hutu Power supported their position on nationalistic grounds. That is, they claimed that they were fighting for the very soul and survival of the Rwandan nation. The hardliners insisted that the RPF, along with most resident Tutsis, wanted to create chaos, take over the government, and kill and repress Hutus.

"Wake Others Up"

To get these messages of fear, anger, and urgency out to the people, the hardliners wasted no time in organizing themselves. In addition to large rallies and word of mouth, they pushed their ideas in *Kangura*, a widely distributed newspaper. Its name translates as "wake others up." Its editor, radical Hutu journalist Hassan Ngeze, also presented the Hutu Power agenda on Rwanda's largest radio station, Radio Television Libre des Mille Collines (RTLM).

Ngeze became famous for writing the "Hutu Ten Commandments," which developed into a major feature of the Hutu Power movement. First introduced in 1990, it consists of a list of anti-Tutsi maxims, sayings, or rules. The first states:

> Every Hutu should know that a Tutsi woman, whoever she is, works for the interest of her Tutsi ethnic group. As a result, we shall consider a traitor any Hutu who marries a Tutsi woman, befriends a Tutsi woman, [or] employs a Tutsi woman as a secretary or a concubine [live-in mistress].[28]

The second rule follows up on the first by advocating that Hutu women are invariably better wives, mothers, and secretaries than Tutsi women. Other maxims on the list claim that all Tutsis are dishonest; that no Hutu should lend to or borrow from a Tutsi; that all important economic, political, and military jobs in the country should go exclusively

Hassan Ngeze became the Hutus' chief propagandist and wrote the "Hutu Ten Commandments," a list of anti-Tutsi ideology and rules.

to Hutus; that Hutus should control education; that no Hutu should ever show mercy to a Tutsi; and that Hutus should aggressively spread and preach these rules to other Hutus.

Ngeze's commandments played a key role in further inflaming the anti-Tutsi hatred that already existed in Rwanda and helped to make Hutu Power a powerful tool and weapon. Particularly dangerous was Ngeze's warning that Tutsis should never receive any mercy. It was destined to make the coming massacres larger and more brutal than they might otherwise have been.

Highly Efficient Organization

Lone journalists, politicians, and other popular figures who stirred up anti-Tutsi hatred were certainly effective. But many experts think that by themselves they would not have been sufficient to instigate and support a countrywide killing spree in which large segments of the population took part. What seems to have sealed the Tutsis' fate was the fact that large numbers of government officials and military personnel took part in both planning and executing the genocide.

Moreover, a key factor was that these conspirators were highly organized and aggressive. In prior years, efficient government organization had been used effectively to help the citizenry. So it was not very difficult to switch gears and use the same official apparatus to harm large numbers of people. Human Rights Watch, a human rights organization, explains,

> In the past, the Rwandan government had often mobilized the population for campaigns of various kinds, such as to end illiteracy, to vaccinate children, or to improve the status of women. It had executed these efforts through the existing administrative and political hierarchies, requiring agents to go beyond their usual duties for a limited period of time for some national goal of major importance.

A Song of Hate

After the signing of the Arusha Accords in August 1993, many Hutus accused President Juvénal Habyarimana of being a traitor for giving too many concessions to the Tutsi "enemy." Soon afterward, a song condemning the so-called Hutu turncoats became popular in the country. Some of its words are:

> I Hate these Hutus, these arrogant Hutus, braggarts, who scorn other Hutus, dear comrades. . . .
>
> I hate these Hutus, these de-Hutuized Hutus, who have disowned their identity, dear comrades.
>
> I hate these Hutus, these Hutus who march blindly, like imbeciles [idiots], this species of naïve Hutus who are manipulated, and who tear themselves up, joining in a war whose cause they ignore.
>
> I detest these Hutus who are brought to kill . . . and who kill the Hutus, dear comrades.

Simon Bikindi, "I Hate These Hutus," Genocide in Rwanda. www.trumanwebdesign.com/~catalina/bikindi.htm.

The organizers of the genocide similarly exploited the structures that already existed—administrative, political, and military—and called upon [official] personnel to execute a campaign to kill Tutsi, [along with any] Hutu presumed to oppose Hutu Power. Through these three channels, the organizers were able to reach all Rwandans and to incite or force most Hutu into acquiescing in [accepting] or participating in the slaughter. . . . Individuals from other sectors, [including] the church, the business community, the university, schools, and hospitals backed the efforts of the officials [out of tradition or habit].[29]

The existing, highly structured governmental ladder of authority that stretched from the national capital down to the local neighborhoods was not the only tool the hard-liners planned to use against the Tutsis. They also began creating civilian forces that they could call on to do their bidding. Organized by the military, these included both neighborhood patrols and militias made up of young Hutu men. (A militia is a group of civilians temporarily pressed into military service.) The well-trained presidential guards also had a hand in training some members of the militias.

Youth militias were not new in Rwanda. The leading single government party already had its own, the *Interahamwe*, meaning "those who stand or fight together." Also, most of the recently formed opposition parties had their own militias. The Hutu party known as the Coalition for the Defense of the Republic (CDR), for example, had the *Impuzamugambi*, or "those who have the same goal."

The normal function of the members of these groups was to take part in party-sponsored marches, to cheer at party rallies, and to fly party flags. However, it was clear to those in power that these peaceful duties could easily be replaced with violent ones. So beginning in 1993, mostly in secret, some of the militias were steadily transformed into paramilitary organizations. The exact extent of their participation in and impact on the genocide remains somewhat unclear. But there is no doubt that they willingly took part, seeing it as a patriotic duty. The leader of the *Interahamwe* later told an investigative reporter: "The government authorizes us. We go in behind the army. We watch them and learn. . . . We have to defend our country. The government authorizes us to defend ourselves by taking up clubs, machetes and whatever guns we could find."[30]

This statement illustrates how low-tech the weapons carried by most members of the militia were. The words "whatever guns we could find" is particularly revealing. The reality was that most of the relatively few modern guns that then existed in Rwanda were in the hands of army soldiers. So in training the militia, the military instructed the recruits to use whatever weapons and other objects they could find that could be used to kill someone. In turn,

Rwandan youth undergo militia training. Both the Hutus and the Tutsis relied on youth soldiers armed with anything they could find.

when organizing local young men to form death squads, the militiamen gave similar orders. A member of one of these squads later recalled:

> Lots of *Interahamwe* had arrived [in our village] in trucks and buses, all jostling and honking on the roads. It was like a city traffic jam. . . . That day [some] misinformed guys had come to the meeting without bringing a [weapon]. The *Interahamwe* lectured them. They said it would pass this once, but had better not happen twice. They

told them to arm themselves with branches and stones [if they lacked machetes].[31]

Newspapers and Radio

In addition to efficient organization and the training of militant youth militias, the Hutu-controlled government carried on a major and sinister campaign of propaganda. With few exceptions, it consisted of exaggerations and outright lies intended to demonize the Tutsis and instill fear among ordinary Hutus. Magazines and newspapers, like Ngeze's

Kangura with its anti-Tutsi command- ments, played important roles in prim- ing the population for mass violence. This was partly because some of these publications were very widely distribut- ed. According to Human Rights Watch:

> The newspapers were published and sold in the capital, but urban workers who often went home for weekends carried copies of the bet- ter-known newspapers out to the hills. Some 66 percent of Rwandans are literate and those who knew how to read were accustomed to reading for others. In many cases, the written word was underscored by cartoons, most of which were so graphic that [their anti-Tutsi themes] could not be misinterpreted.[32]

Even more effective in circulating mis- information were radio broadcasts by RTLM and other stations. Their success as propaganda sources was due largely to the fact that most Rwandans owned radios, often given away free by the gov- ernment. In 1993 and on into 1994, these broadcasts put out a steady stream of slanted news reports, speeches, poems, talk shows, and songs.

Typically the news reports and speeches claimed that the Tutsis of the RPF had committed and were continu- ing to perpetrate awful atrocities. These supposedly brutal acts included killing innocent Hutu civilians. But in reality that charge was rarely true. The radio reports distributed much more false or misleading information, but most Rwan-

dans lacked other independent, reliable news sources that would have exposed the lies.

Other common themes of the broad- casts emphasized that all Tutsis were accomplices of the RPF and that Tutsis were racially inferior, even subhuman. A word repeatedly used to describe the Tutsis, for instance, was *inyenzi*, mean- ing "cockroach." A typical example appeared in one of Ngeze's articles. It reads, "We know where the cockroaches are. If they look for us, they had better watch out." Another, even more threat- ening example is: "What weapons shall we use to conquer the cockroaches once and for all?"[33]

The radio talk shows were also quite effective, in large degree because they were casual in tone, giving the impres- sion of neighbors speaking directly to neighbors. Indeed, as the Human Rights Watch states:

> These broadcasts were like a con- versation among Rwandans who knew each other well and were relaxing over some banana beer or a bottle of Primus [the local beer] in a bar. It was a conversation without a moderator and without any requirements as to the truth of what was said. The people who were there recounted what they had seen or heard during the day. The exchanges covered everything: rumors circulating on the hills, news from the national radio, con- flicts among local political bosses. . . . It was all in fun. Some people

Using Radio to Spread Propaganda

Nazi Germany used radio to create propaganda in the 1930s and 1940s, and the Hutu-controlled Rwandan government adopted the same techniques in the early 1990s. Concordia University scholar Frank Chalk explains:

Radio has been one of the great forces for social and political mobilization in the twentieth century. [It] was [Nazi propaganda expert] Joseph Goebbels [pronounced GER-blz] who brought its use to perfection. Goebbels subsidized the production and distribution by German manufacturers of millions of cheap radios for German homes and ordered the installation of loudspeakers to broadcast Nazi radio news bulletins and speeches in factories and public places, where listeners were observed by so-called radio wardens. . . . In Rwanda, radios and batteries to power them were too expensive for most peasants to afford until the 1980s, when the Rwandan government obtained foreign aid for the purchase and distribution of radios, arguing that they were necessary to promote the dissemination of modern farming technology. The radios were then given away during election campaigns. . . . The Rwandan government, like Germany's under the Nazis, invested heavily in powerful radio transmitters and repeater facilities to blanket the country with radio broadcasts.

Frank Chalk, "Radio Propaganda and Genocide," Montreal Institute for Genocide and Human Rights Studies, November 1999. http://migs.concordia.ca/occpapers/radio_pr.html.

Nazi propaganda master Joseph Goebbels prepares to give a speech on radio in 1938.

left the bar, others came in, the conversation went on or stopped if it got too late, and the next day it took up again after work.[34]

The problem was that these supposedly impromptu conversations were actually carefully crafted to reinforce progovernment, anti-Tutsi messages.

Meanwhile the poems and songs on the radio also helped to spread messages of fear and hate. Particularly popular was pop musician Simon Bikindi's tune "I Hate These Hutus." Its mean-spirited lyrics condemn moderate Hutus who do not despise and want to get rid of Tutsis.

The Power of Propaganda

A number of historians have pointed out that no one knows for sure how many and which of the pregenocide media campaigns against the Tutsis contributed to the subsequent genocide. Some studies conducted after the mass killings suggest that some of the Hutu who participated in the murders did not do so specifically because they believed the propaganda. However, there seems little doubt that at least some of the well-orchestrated misinformation programs worked as they were intended to. One study conducted by University of Wisconsin scholar Scott Straus looked at how Ngeze's anti-Tutsi rules affected average Hutus during the run-up of the genocide. Of those individuals who answered his survey, the ones who had read or heard about the rules "were among the most violent," Straus reported. Those familiar with the document, "presumably those most tuned into the most racist propaganda, were the most prone to initiate and drive the violence."[35]

Also, there is widespread agreement that certain speeches and slogans by well-known politicians and government officials were effective over time in escalating Hutu hatred of Tutsis. Often cited is a speech given by noted Hutu prefecture official Leon Mugesera. In it he called the Tutsis "foreigners from Ethiopia," an African country lying well north of Rwanda. "We will send them home by the shortest route," Mugesera said, by "throwing them into the Nyabarongo River." These were code words for killing the Tutsis. But in case there were any listeners who did not get that message, the speaker quickly followed up with words whose meaning was quite unmistakable: "We must act. [We must] wipe them all out." Minutes later he added: "Know that the person whose throat you do not cut now will be the one who will cut yours [later]."[36]

Much of the language from the RTLM broadcasts was no less direct, offensive, and powerful. In the early months of 1994, with anti-Tutsi messages becoming more and more explicit, one Hutu boldly spoke of exterminating "them," by which of course he meant the Tutsis: "We will fight them and we will vanquish them, this is more than certain. All doubt is impossible and if they don't watch out they will be exterminated. . . . They are a clique representing only a small percentage of the population." Another agitated Hutu speaker said that the Tutsi minority was "en route to

Radio propagandist Leon Mugesera's speeches, filled with code words that meant kill the Tutsis, greatly escalated Hutu hatred of the Tutsis.

extinction in Rwanda." Then he asked, "Are these people going to continue to kill themselves off, to engage in this suicidal battle against the majority—won't this truly be the end of them?" A man in still another radio broadcast compared the Tutsis to cows in a slaughterhouse and said, "I don't know if they have been slaughtered today or will be slaughtered tonight."[37]

A Recipe for Disaster?

For months, General Romeo Dallaire, the Canadian officer in charge of the United Nations Assistance Mission for Rwanda (UNAMIR) forces in Rwanda, listened to such broadcasts with mounting apprehension and foreboding. He and his men were there to keep the peace as best as they could. The question that continually gnawed at him was whether their best efforts would be good enough. There were millions of Hutus, but far fewer Tutsis and even fewer foreign troops in the country. Dallaire was well aware that, under the right circumstances, this could be a recipe for a disaster of huge proportions. He later wrote:

It was evident to me and others [in UNAMIR] that hardline voices, pushing ethnic arguments and fears, were beginning to dominate the discussions, and there was an increasingly violent tone to political discourse, fed by the broadcasts of RTLM. The atmosphere in Kigali was becoming tense.[38]

During the 1993 Christmas holidays, Dallaire and his wife threw a small dinner

"Another Kick in the Butt"

Rwandan hotel manager Paul Rusesabagina was treated poorly by Hutu military thugs in the months during which Hutu Power was spreading and laying the foundation for the genocide to come. For weeks he had been berated for not wearing a medallion, showing the likeness of the Hutu dictator, Juvénal Habyarimana. Rusesabagina recalls,

A black car arrived at the front door [and] I was escorted over. They told me I now had earned "an appointment" at the office of the president. I followed them there in a hotel car and allowed myself to be led into a side office, where I was screamed at for several hours. "You do not respect the boss, our father!" they screamed at me. "What did I do wrong?" I asked, although I knew. "You stupid man, you did not wear your medals! Why not?" "I don't see the benefit in doing that," I said. It went around and around like this before they kicked me out of the office—with a literal foot planted on my butt—and a command to be back the next morning. And the next day, they screamed at me for hours and gave me another kick in the butt before they let me go. It went on like this every day for a month.

Paul Rusesabagina, with Tom Zoellner, *An Ordinary Man*. Thorndike, ME: Center Point, 2006, p. 88.

party for some of their fellow Canadians then stationed in Rwanda. One of them, Helene Pinsky, was married to a moderate Rwandan politician, one of several who had been invited to the gathering. In recent months, Dallaire later remembered, she had done her best to ignore the bitter propaganda. An optimist, she was certain that, with the signing of the Arusha Accords and the arrival of the UNAMIR forces, the situation in Rwanda was actually improving. She insisted, "there would only be bright days ahead as decency and respect for human rights took hold in the nation."[39] None present at the party foresaw how utterly mistaken she was. Nor could they have guessed that within a few months every Rwandan in attendance that evening would be dead.

Chapter Four

The Butchery Begins

With so much earnest, angry talk of extermination and slaughter appearing in print and on the radio in Rwanda, some observers, both inside and outside the country, detected a dangerous situation looming. They were concerned about what the government hard-liners and others who hated the Tutsis might do. In particular, they worried that some of those in power might act on the threats made in the increasingly ugly bouts of propaganda.

Indeed, ominous indications that this was about to happen began to emerge early in 1994. On January 8 President Habyarimana and representatives of the RPF were scheduled to meet in the main government building in Kigali. There was to be a ceremony there to swear in the members of a transitional government provided for in the Arusha Accords. (Of the twenty-one cabinet positions in that temporary government,

five each had been granted to the president's party and the RPF; the other posts had been divided among various other parties.)

The ceremony did not take place as planned, however. As the representatives began to approach the building, a large and angry crowd of civilians materialized seemingly out of nowhere. The protestors were armed with machetes and clubs. They shouted and threatened, focusing nearly all their rage on the moderate politicians and RPF members. Similar heated crowds gathered in other parts of the capital at the same time.

Romeo Dallaire and other members of UNAMIR who witnessed the commotion outside the government building immediately sensed that the demonstration was both staged and well planned. Furthermore, they recognized members of the presidential guard in the crowd. They were wearing civilian clothes and carefully directing and inciting the protestors. It was all too clear to Dallaire that the hard-liners were intent on foiling the implementation of the Arusha Accords and a new, fairer government.

In addition, Dallaire realized that, if so ordered, the armed protestors would have hacked or beaten the politicians to death without hesitation. The hardliners' ability to manipulate huge crowds of potential killers filled him and the other UN peacekeepers with dread. They worried that large-scale outbreaks of violence might erupt in the near future. As it turned out, this troubling concern was well founded. Rwanda was about to descend into an orgy of barbarity that would rank among the bloodiest events in modern history.

The Warning

Not long after the failed swearing-in ceremony, Dallaire found even more cause for apprehension. On January 10 he was approached in secret by a member of the *Interahamwe*. This individual, known only as Jean-Pierre, the code name given to him by Dallaire and his aides, had originally been a member of the presidential guard. Recently he had been ordered to begin working as a trainer of new recruits for the *Interahamwe*. In this capacity he soon become disturbed by what was happening outside the public eye. Dallaire later recalled:

He and others like him were ordered to have the cells [groups of militiamen] under their command make lists of the Tutsis in their

various communes. Jean-Pierre suspected that these lists were being made so that, when the time came, the Tutsis . . . could easily be rounded up and exterminated. Jean-Pierre said that he hated the RPF and saw them as an enemy of Rwanda, but he was horrified that he had been drawn into a plan to create a series of highly efficient death squads that, when turned loose on the population, could kill a thousand Tutsis in Kigali within twenty minutes of receiving the order. He described in detail how the *Interahamwe* were being trained at army bases, [including a] course that placed special emphasis on killing techniques. The young men were [then] returned to their communes and ordered to make lists of Tutsis and await the call to arms.[40]

The horrified UNAMIR leader became even more disturbed when the informant told him that Hutu hard-liners were also planning to murder some of the Belgians under his command. On January 11 Dallaire quietly notified his superiors at UN headquarters in New York City. He recommended that Jean-Pierre and his family be given protection and evacuated from Rwanda. Dallaire also said he was convinced that "the president does not have full control over all elements of his old party/faction."[41] In addition, the hard-liners had accumulated large numbers of guns, explosives, and other arms in a secret storage facility. Dallaire told his superiors that he was

UN Rwandan forces commander Romeo Dallaire, left, received instructions from UN superiors to avoid the use of force in Kigali, as it "might lead to unanticipated repercussions." The decision insured that a bloodbath would begin.

considering raiding that facility as soon as possible.

The UN officials Dallaire had contacted responded to him later the same day. To his surprise and disappointment, their message began:

> We have carefully reviewed the situation in the light of your [coded communication, and] we cannot agree to the operation [the proposed raid on the arms cache], as it clearly goes beyond the mandate

entrusted to UNAMIR under [UN] resolution 872. However, on the assumption that you are convinced that the information provided by the informant is absolutely reliable, we request you to undertake the initiatives described in the following paragraphs.

Among these initiatives, Dallaire was instructed to inform President Habyarimana of what Jean-Pierre had said. The president was to be warned that if any

Like Sacks of Potatoes

In the following excerpt from his book, Shake Hands with the Devil: The Failure of Humanity in Rwanda, *General Romeo Dallaire describes the distressing sight of the bodies of the ten murdered Belgian soldiers arriving at a local hospital.*

Several soldiers, including a number of wounded, were milling around the entrance [to the hospital]. . . . At the back door an officer told [us] that the bodies of the Belgians were at the far end of the large courtyard in front of the morgue. The word *bodies* hit me right in the heart and shocked me for a moment. I heard gasps and other sounds of disbelief all around me. They were all dead. . . . At first I saw what seemed to be sacks of potatoes to the right of the morgue door. It slowly resolved in my vision into a heap of mangled and bloodied white flesh in tattered Belgian para-commando uniforms. The men were piled on top of each other. [We] counted them twice: eleven soldiers. In the end it turned out to be ten.

Romeo Dallaire, *Shake Hands with the Devil: The Failure of Humanity in Rwanda.* New York: Carroll and Graf, 2003, p. 255.

violence erupted in Kigali, it would be reported to the UN Security Council. Also, Dallaire should brief the ambassadors of Belgium, France, and the United States. The message concluded with these words of caution: "We wish to stress . . . that the overriding consideration is the need to avoid entering into a course of action that might lead to the use of force and unanticipated repercussions [outcomes]."[42]

The contents of the message upset Dallaire a great deal. He knew that the orders he had been given would do nothing to stop the violence that he suspected was imminent. "I was absolutely beside myself with frustration,"[43] he later recalled. For several days he repeatedly made phone calls to his superiors, trying to make them change their minds. But his efforts were to no avail.

Assassination, Blame Game, and Coup

As it turned out, Dallaire was right to worry that a calamity of huge and terrible proportions was about to happen. What he could not then foresee was the unexpected event that would initiate that calamity. On Wednesday evening, April 6, 1994, President Habyarimana was in a plane returning from an important meeting of African heads of state in Dar es Salaam, Tanzania's largest city.

With him were Burundi's president, Cyprien Ntaryamira; the chief of staff of Rwanda's army, General Nsabimana; and other high-placed Africans. As the plane began to descend toward the runway, it was struck by several ground-to-air missiles that sped from a hidden position nearby. The explosion and subsequent crash killed everyone onboard.

The identity of the assassins remains unknown. Rwandan soldiers soon found the rocket launchers that had fired the missiles. But the government officials who investigated the attack said they had no idea who was behind it. Not surprisingly, the leading Hutu hard-liners in the government immediately blamed the RPF for bringing down the plane and killing the president. However, as a number of informed observers later pointed out, both the RPF and vari- ous high-placed Hutus had reasons for wanting to kill Habyarimana. According to Human Rights Watch:

The RPF, politicians opposed to Habyarimana, and the circle of his own supporters all might have wanted the Rwandan president dead and could have found the means to bring down his plane. RPF might have launched the missiles . . . because they believed that Habyarimana would never permit the Accords to be implemented. [Or powerful Hutus, including] some in Habyarimana's own circle, might have wanted to eliminate him to avoid the installation of a new government that would diminish their power [and] some feared that he would return from

Rwanda Patriotic Front rebels inspect the wreckage of the plane in which President Habyarimana and Barundi's president Cyprien Ntaromira were killed on April 6, 1994.

Dar es Salaam ready to implement the Accords. . . . Habyarimana's chief of staff, says that the president had, in fact, made such a decision and had told him to bring an announcement to that effect to the airport when he came to welcome him home. The expectation that the new government was about to be installed would have increased pressure on Hutu Power advocates to launch the violence immediately, whether fully prepared or not.[44]

Upon Habyarimana's death, the hard-liners in the government rapidly took measures that they hoped would place them in power. Later in the same evening of the assassination, Théoneste Bagosora, an extreme hard-liner in a high post of the ministry of defense, called a meeting of the leading army officers. He insisted that the army should take over the government immediately. However, the moderates among the officers, who outnumbered the extremists in the group, disagreed. They pointed out that the prime minister, Agathe Uwilingiyimana, was still alive. She should take charge, they argued. The moderates also said they thought it best to go ahead with the Arusha Accords and to work in good faith with Dallaire and his UN peacekeepers. Hearing what had happened at the meeting, the somewhat relieved Dallaire sent ten Belgian soldiers to guard the prime minister.

To the UNAMIR commander's regret, his hopes for a peaceful solution to the crisis were swiftly dashed. Later that night,

in a stunning series of events, Bagosora and his cronies turned on the moderates and seized power. First, the hard-liners surrounded the radio stations and Prime Minister Uwilingiyimana's house. Then they captured the ten Belgian soldiers guarding her. Not long afterward, Bagosora ordered the murders of Uwilingiyimana and the Belgians. The latter were first brutally tortured, then shot repeatedly, and finally hacked to pieces. As the coup continued, the hard-liners ordered the killing of all the chief moderate politicians. One historian writes:

Within hours of the assassination and after losing the immediate initiative to the moderates . . . the hardliners struck back. They did so violently and by using the [connections in the government and the army] they had cultivated during the months prior to the assassination.[45]

Chaos in Kigali

In a radio broadcast the next morning (April 7), Bagosora announced that the army was presently restoring order. He also made it clear that the hardliners were now in charge. On April 8, he made a deal with Joseph Nzirorera, head of the largest Hutu political party, which resulted in the formation of a new government. Bagosora and his chief supporters chose Theodore Sindikubwabo, an elderly politician with little influence, as the country's new president. Clearly, Sindikubwabo was a figurehead with no real power, as the hard-liners were com-

Death of Rwanda's Prime Minister

On April 6, 1994, Hutu hard-liners murdered Rwanda's prime minister, Agathe Uwilingiy-imana. Eyewitness Thomas Kamilindi recalls:

Two armored vehicles arrived at Prime Minister Uwilingiyimana's house with a large contingent of soldiers. The soldiers attacked her residence, and the troops that should have protected her, including the troops from UNAMIR [the UN peacekeepers], were overwhelmed. The prime minister hid with her family, but the government soldiers eventually found her and pulled her out from under a bed where she was trying to hide. . . . The soldiers took her and her family into another room. . . . They finally shot her to death in front of her whole family. Her husband and her mother were also shot, but her children managed to escape, were evacuated by UNAMIR, and are now being sheltered somewhere in Europe.

Quoted in John A. Berry and Carol P. Berry, *Genocide in Rwanda: A Collective Memory*. Washington, DC: Howard University Press, p. 14.

Prime Minister Agathe Uwilingiyimana is pictured with her two children, who witnessed her murder.

pletely in control. He later admitted that he did not want the job but accepted it because he feared he would be killed if he said no.

Meanwhile, Kigali and the areas surrounding it were in a state of unrest and chaos. Dallaire later described the unruly scene on April 8. He said that many fearful civilians fled the capital while members of the *Interahamwe* and other youth militias were setting up roadblocks. The roadblocks were intended to corral the crowds long enough for the Tutsis within them to be singled out. Once these Tutsis were herded into groups, the militiamen immediately began murdering them. The killers used machetes, guns, or whatever other weapons they could find.

The exact moment the massacres began is unknown. The killing appears to have started on April 8, but some Rwandan sources claim that a number of Tutsis in Kigali were slain the day before. What is more certain is that these murders were still, relatively speaking, on a small scale. The genocide began in earnest on April 12. On that day Bagosora and other hard-liners openly called on the country's Hutu population to commence killing Tutsis.

Remarkably Well Organized

From that moment on, a deadly conspiracy went into operation. Key members of the national government and army, along with many thousands of militiamen and local citizens, worked together to carry out mass killings. To help incite and perpetuate the awful process, radio

The Tutsi massacres started in April 1994. Hundreds of Tutsis were killed at the Rukara Catholic Mission.

The Interahamwe *murdered Tutsi teachers and schoolchildren at Nyarubuye on May 15, 1994.*

once more proved an efficient tool, this time brutally so. Hotel manager Paul Rusesabagina remembers how broadcasts from Rwanda's largest radio station, Radio Television Libre des Mille Collines (RTLM) repeatedly ordered the death squads to carry out their grisly work:

The radio was instructing all its listeners to murder their neighbors. "Do your work," I heard the announcer say. "Clean your neighborhood of brush. Cut the tall trees." . . . The "tall trees" was an unmistakable reference to the Tutsis. "Clean your neighborhood of brush" meant that rebel army sym-

pathizers might be hiding among Tutsi families and so the entire family should be "cleaned" to be on the safe side. . . . Here at last were the bones under the skin. All the anti-Tutsi rhetoric put out on the air over the previous six months had blossomed into what they were now actually saying out loud: Kill your neighbors! Murder your friends![46]

One might assume that Hutus who heard these homicidal orders and decided to obey them would do so in a disorganized, confused, and hectic manner. However, just the opposite occurred. Thanks to the secret planning and training that the hard-liners had implemented

The Butchery Begins ■ 61

in the previous months, the massacres were remarkably well organized. This was especially true considering the large numbers of people involved. According to Peace Pledge Union, an international peace group, most of the killers were members of "civilian death squads" who had been "trained to massacre." The group also describes how well the killers were organized:

> Transport and fuel supplies [and even food and drinks] were [set aside in supply bases] for the *Interahamwe*. Even remote areas were catered for. Where the killers encountered opposition, the Army backed them up with manpower and weapons. The [government] provided Hutu Power's supporting organization; politicians, officials, intellectuals, and professional soldiers deliberately incited (and where necessary bribed) the killers to do their work. Local officials assisted in rounding up victims and making suitable places available for their slaughter.[47]

Indeed, the efficient organization in all levels of Rwanda's government significantly contributed to the rising death toll. The exact number of people killed in the first few days of the genocide is uncertain. But those who later examined these events in detail agree that it was at least several thousand. In Kigali and the larger towns, members of the *Interahamwe* and other militia went from building to building and from house to house.

If they found ordinary Hutus, they did nothing and moved on. In contrast, if they found Tutsis or well-known Hutus known to be moderates, they forced their way in and butchered them. In the meantime, frightened Tutsis and Hutus alike ran for their lives. Some tried to escape into the countryside; others did the opposite and streamed from their villages into the cities.

Outsiders' Reactions to the Crisis

In the midst of this turmoil and bloodletting, Dallaire and his UN forces found themselves at a frustrating and tragic impasse. They had guns, trucks, and helicopters, and they wanted desperately to intervene and try to stop the killing. But the mandate, or mission rules, they had been given by their UN superiors allowed them only to monitor what was happening. They were strictly forbidden from getting involved in the fighting. As a result, at first there was little they could do, and some Rwandans viewed them as useless. Early in the crisis, one Kigali businessman phoned UNAMIR headquarters and asked for an armed escort through the capital. To his surprise and disgust, he was told: "No way. There are roadblocks all over Kigali, and people are being killed on the roads."[48]

Another group of outsiders, the armed troops of the RPF, lacked the restraints that had been placed on Dallaire's forces. As the crisis began, about six hundred RPF soldiers were stationed in Kigali as part of the agreement recently struck in Arusha. They now came under attack by

An Unexpected Avalanche

The United States and other major Western nations were taken almost totally by surprise by the enormous and rapid outbreak of violence in Rwanda in 1994, including the assassination of President Juvénal Habyarimana. This was evident on May 3, 1994, when Madeleine Albright, U.S. representative to the United Nations, met with U.S. congressmen about an unrelated issue. She said,

But let me just tell you that on the Rwanda thing, it is my sense that to a great extent the Security Council and the UN missed the boat. We are now dealing with a situation way beyond anything that anybody expected. And as I mentioned earlier, what happened was that we were on one process where a smaller United Nations force, we felt, could deal with some of the issues in the area, and then all of a sudden with the shoot-down of this airplane with the two presidents [Habyarimana and Cyprien Ntaryamira of Burundi, who was also on the plane], it created an avalanche [of violence].

Quoted in PBS, "100 Days of Slaughter: A Chronology of U.S./U.N. Actions," www.pbs.org/wgbh/pages/frontline/shows/evil/etc/slaughter.html.

Rwandan army units, which surrounded them. In the weeks that followed, the RPF troops bravely launched their own small offensives when they could. All the while they resigned themselves to trying to hold out until more RPF forces could reach the capital and rescue them. On April 8 the RPF launched a major offensive from Uganda designed to do just that.

That same day, people in nations around the world began to hear news reports about the escalating violence in Rwanda. The most immediate concern of governments of other countries was the safety of their citizens who might be living in or visiting Rwanda. In the United States, President Bill Clinton tried to reassure the American public that U.S. citizens visiting Rwanda would be safe, saying:

I mention it only because there are a sizable number of Americans there and it is a very tense situation. And I just want to assure the families of those who are there that we are doing everything we possibly can to be on top of the situation to take all the appropriate steps to try to assure the safety of our citizens there.[49]

Although this and similar U.S. government statements expressed sincere concern, it was unlikely that the United States would take any overt, aggressive action in Rwanda. Certainly, President Clinton and his advisers were not willing to send troops to become entangled in the Rwandan civil war. This was partly because the United States had no important strategic interests in Rwanda, such as oil, and Rwanda posed no threats of terrorism. Also, several U.S. soldiers had recently been brutally murdered in another African nation, Somalia. So neither U.S. leaders nor the public they served were willing to risk any more American lives in Africa.

As a result, official statements by U.S. leaders about the Rwandan crisis tended to be vague, pacifying, and masked what those leaders really thought. For example, when reporters asked U.S. State Department spokesperson Christine Shelley if she considered the ongoing killings in Rwanda to be genocide, she replied, "The use of the term 'genocide' has a very precise legal meaning, although it's not strictly a legal determination. There are other factors in there as well."[50] This roundabout answer ignored the fact that a secret State Department intelligence

UN soldiers guard French and Belgian civilians as they evacuate from the Kigali region in April 1994. The UN's withdrawal meant Bagosora's mass killings would continue.

report had already labeled the mass murders in Rwanda as genocide. However, American officials knew full well that if they used that word in public, they would then have to explain why they were not planning to intervene in Rwanda and stop the massacres.

The same reluctance to get involved in the growing crisis in Rwanda prevailed in other national governments around the world. For the leaders of these countries, this approach or policy was reinforced when the shocking news came that the Belgian soldiers guarding the Rwandan prime minister had been savagely murdered. Reacting to this and other growing violence, the UN reduced its forces in Rwanda from 2,500 to 250 on April 21. Moreover, almost all of the foreign governments that had citizens or other interests in Rwanda also reacted by withdrawing from the country.

This virtual retreat on the part of the UN and foreign nations played right into the hands of Bagosora and the other hard-liners who had seized the reins of Rwanda's government. They realized that if the outside world refused to get involved, they could continue their kill-ing spree unhindered. Human Rights Watch explains:

As the new leaders were consolidating control over military commanders, they profited enormously from the first demonstration of international timidity. UN troops in Rwanda [had no choice but to leave] the local population at the mercy of [the Hutu] assailants. [Rwandan] officers opposed to Bagosora realized that a continuing foreign presence was essential to restricting the killing campaign and appealed to representatives of France, Belgium and the U.S. not to desert Rwanda. But, suspecting the kind of horrors to come, the foreigners had already packed their bags.[51]

Indeed, hundreds of well-trained Belgian, French, and Italian troops hurried to evacuate their own citizens, then left Rwanda with equal swiftness. That meant that for the time being the human targets in the country's ongoing catastrophe were on their own in their desperate fight for survival. Tragically, many of them were destined to lose that fight.

Chapter Five

The Genocide at Its Height

The genocide that began in Rwanda in early April 1994 continued for one hundred days, a little more than three months. During those months, soldiers, members of the militias, and unknown numbers of ordinary civilians went on a horrifying killing spree. Most of the victims were Tutsis, whom the murderers viewed as inferiors, subhumans, and cockroaches. But a number of moderate Hutus were targeted as well.

People were slaughtered in their homes, in the streets, in churches, and in forests, meadows, and swamps in the countryside. In a majority of cases, the killers showed no mercy whatsoever. Men, women, children, and even infants were targeted. The cruelty and extreme disregard for human life the members of the death squads exhibited was sadly and graphically illustrated by the cold-blooded murder of numerous pregnant women. One such victim's sister, Janvier Munyaneza, then fourteen, later remembered how an attacker dragged her sister "onto the grass and struck her once with his club." Then, "a close neighbor, called Hakizma, shouted that she was pregnant. He sliced open her belly with a knife [and] opened her up like a sack. That is what human eyes have seen."[52] Janvier was also hit by a club but managed to survive by pretending to be dead.

Enticing Incentives

When news of the murders reached the outside world, people wondered how the killers could bring themselves to commit such horrific acts. The answer is complex, involving numerous social and other cultural factors peculiar to Rwanda. It also entails the destructive potential of people who had lived for a long time under repressive governments and been conditioned to hate by decades of distorted propaganda.

Putting these complicated and long-term causes for the genocide aside, the more immediate motivations of the Rwandan killers can be fairly easily understood. In large part, they were coldly and efficiently manipulated by their government, which in the wake of President Habyarimana's assassination was controlled by extreme Hutu hard-liners. In many cases, the hard-liners orchestrating the massacres offered poor young men what were widely viewed as enticing incentives. According to Human Rights Watch, government officials

delivered food, drink, and other intoxicants, parts of military uni-

forms and small payments in cash to hungry, jobless young men. They encouraged cultivators to pillage farm animals, crops, and such building materials as doors, windows and roofs. Even more important in this land-hungry society, they promised cultivators the fields left vacant by Tutsi victims. To entrepreneurs [enterprising businessmen] and members of the local elite, they granted houses, vehicles, control of a small business, or such rare goods as television sets or computers. Many poor young men responded readily to the promise of rewards. Of the nearly 60 percent of

Hutu authorities offered many incentives to recruit jobless Rwandan youth into killing squads, enticing them with food, drink, intoxicants, cash, and uniforms.

Rwandans under the age of twenty, tens of thousands had little hope of obtaining the land needed to establish their own households or the jobs necessary to provide for a family. Such young men, including many displaced by the [Rwandan civil] war and living in camps near the capital, provided many of the early recruits to the [killing squads] in the days immediately after the genocide began.[53]

Journalist Philip Gourevitch also uncovered evidence of government hard-liners offering various valuable goods and services to entice angry and in some cases greedy young men to kill. He writes, "As an added incentive to the killers, Tutsis' belongings were parceled out in advance—the radio, the couch, the goat, the opportunity to rape a young girl." Yet land, other articles of property, and the illicit use of young women were not the only material incentives offered by the authorities. According to Gourevitch, "A councilwoman in one Kigali neighborhood was reported to have offered fifty Rwandan francs apiece (about thirty cents at the time) for severed Tutsi heads, a practice known as 'selling cabbages.'"[54]

Thus, for some desperately poor Rwandans, money became a potent inducement to commit murder. The government not only sometimes paid bounties to the killers, it also imposed monetary fines on them if they refused to take part in the massacres. One such killer, who called himself Adalbert, later said, "The fines varied. [It] was one thousand or two thousand francs [but] it could go as high as five thousand. . . . At first these fines were very punishing for a farmer because of his poverty." Another mass murderer agreed, saying, "Many killed simply to get around their poverty. If they went along with the killings, they did not risk fines."[55]

Transformed into Killers

Others who joined the death squads did not need material incentives to become killers. Many of them saw themselves as patriotic supporters of President Habyarimana. When he was assassinated, they jumped to the conclusion that Tutsis were responsible and decided to retaliate. One of these young men, who killed some of his own neighbors in the region of Kayove, in western Rwanda, later described his reasons for taking part in the mass killings:

During the night [of April 6, 1994], a neighbor came to tell me that he had just heard on the radio that Habyarimana had been shot. In my mind, I understood right away that the Tutsis were responsible. I was angry, and I said to myself, "It is true. The Tutsis are mean.". . . I found that peasants had set up roadblocks. It was then they said, "No Tutsi can remain in our sector.". . . [On] the 8th, we heard a woman had been killed, we heard that in the other sectors people were being killed. So we too attacked those [Tutsis] who were our neighbors.[56]

Haunted by His Deeds

Although many of the killers in the Rwandan genocide later expressed little or no regret or guilt, at least a few were psychologically damaged by their participation in the mass murders. A survivor, teacher Innocent Rwililiza, later recalled the case of a killer who was long haunted by his crimes.

I learned [of] a killer who had buried his Tutsi neighbor completely alive in a hole behind the man's house. Eight months later, he felt himself called by his victim in a dream. He went back to that garden, he dug up the dirt, unearthed the corpse, and got himself arrested. Since then, in the prison, he wanders day and night with that man's skull in a plastic bag he holds tight in his hand. He cannot let go of the bag even to eat. He is haunted to the last extremity.

Quoted in Jean Hatzfeld, *Life Laid Bare: The Survivors in Rwanda Speak*. New York: Other Press, 2000, pp. 113–14.

Another excuse that some of the killers cited was that, at least in part, they succumbed to a group mentality. As long as the group was killing, individuals in the group no longer thought or reasoned for themselves, and over time they got used to committing acts normally seen as heinous. Jospeh-Desiré Bitero, who was thirty-one when he joined a death squad, remembers:

It became a madness that went on all by itself. You raced ahead, or you got out of the way to escape being run over, but you followed the crowd. . . . Doing the same thing every day meant that we didn't have to think about what we were doing. [We] hunted because it

was the order of the day, until the day was over. Our arms ruled our heads.[57]

One of Bitero's fellow killers, Pio Mutungirehe, says he also became part of a deadly mob mind-set. After repeatedly and mechanically committing murder, Mutungirehe felt himself drawn into a primitive, barbaric mental state that in prior years he never would have thought possible. He explains:

We no longer saw a human being when we turned up a Tutsi in the swamps. [The] hunt was savage, the hunters were savage, the prey was savage—savagery took over the mind. Not only had we become criminals, we had become a ferocious species in a barbarous world. . . . It [was as] if I had let another individual take on my own living appearance. [Probably] someone outside this situation . . . cannot have an inkling of that strangeness of mind.[58]

Merciless Slaughter

Whatever their reasons for participating in the mass murders, those who did so were most often methodical and ruthless. Often they calmly walked from one Tutsi-owned house to another and butchered whoever was home at the time. In other instances, the death squads went to larger buildings, such as schools and churches, where many Tutsis had gathered in hopes that there might be safety in numbers. But such security was only an illusion. The militiamen and other killers were actually glad when their victims congregated together in groups, because it allowed them to kill more people in less time.

One example of such large group slayings occurred in mid-April 1994 at a church in the commune of Nyange, in western Rwanda. There, the mayor, police inspector, and parish priest, all Hutus, conspired to exterminate as many local Tutsis as possible. First the three got some Hutu thugs to terrorize the Tutsis and drive them from their homes. Then the conspirators, pretending to help the frightened people, urged them to seek safety in the local church.

At least two thousand Tutsis crowded into the building. Then the mayor and his two high-placed accomplices called in some soldiers and members of the *Interahamwe*, who surrounded the church and further terrorized those trapped inside. Finally the attackers singled out Anatase Nkinamubanzi, a Rwandan construction worker who wanted no part of the brutal affair. As he later testified, he was forced to use his Caterpillar bulldozer to destroy the structure while the Tutsis were still inside:

I was given instructions [to] bring the church down. . . . As I did not move fast enough for their liking, an *interahamwe* standing next to the judicial police officer stuck a knife in my shoulder saying "You, you get to work." So I was bleeding when I started to work. There were about two thousand people in the church. . . . The soldiers started shooting inside the church before the bulldozing began. Some people died from the gunfire and some of the walls of the church had been damaged by the time we started bulldozing. When the bulldozing began, some people ran out of the church in terror. But the [killers] forced them into the church by attacking them with machetes. . . . The church was completely destroyed [and] there was only rubble and dead bodies. But the soldiers were kept there to make sure that no one came to dig out any survivors.[59]

An even larger and more lethal example of such merciless slaughter took place in another church. The Nyarubuye Catholic Church was located in Kibungo Province, about 60 miles (97km) east of Kigali. On April 15, in what came to be called the Nyarubuye massacre, large numbers of Tutsis and Hutu moderates fled their homes and gathered in the church, the interior of which was extremely spacious. The exact number of victims remains unknown, but estimates

The Hutu killers knew no limits in their indiscriminate slaughter of Tutsis, including pregnant women and young children.

A Grim Discovery

Philip Gourevitch, author of one of the most highly acclaimed books about the Rwandan genocide, visited the country thirteen months after the tragedy and made a grim discovery.

There's a rocky hill called Nyarubuye with a church where many Tutsis were slaughtered. [We] flew [there] in a United Nations helicopter, traveling low over the hills in the morning mists. . . . I stepped up into the open doorway of a classroom. At least fifty mostly decomposed cadavers [bodies] covered the floor, wadded in clothing, their belongings strewn about and smashed. Macheted skulls had rolled here and there. The dead looked like pictures of the dead. They did not smell. They did not buzz with flies. They had been killed thirteen months earlier, and they hadn't been moved. Skin stuck here and there over the bones, many of which lay scattered away from the bodies, dismembered by the killers, or by scavengers—birds, dogs, bugs. . . . It was still strangely unimaginable. [Those] dead Rwandans will be with me forever, I expect.

Philip Gourevitch, *We Wish to Inform You That Tomorrow We Will Be Killed with Our Families: Stories from Rwanda*, New York: Farrar, Straus and Giroux, 1998, pp. 15–16.

On April 15 the inside of the Nyarubuye church was the scene of a mass slaughter of Tutsis and Hutu moderates. Between 5,000 and 10,000 were hacked to death by Hutu executioners.

run from as low as five thousand to well over ten thousand. As in other attacks on churches, the building was surrounded by Hutu executioners carrying guns, machetes, farm implements, and clubs. At a given signal, they entered the church and systematically began slaughtering those huddled inside. One of the few survivors, Rosine Nshirmiriama, later remembered:

Waiting their turn, mothers, fathers, brothers, sisters and children watched in horror as their families were hacked, slashed, or bludgeoned to death. The lucky ones were shot or decapitated and died instantly, but many, with amputated limbs, were left to die a slow and torturously painful death. People tried in vain to protect their loved ones; mothers sheltered children who clung on, eyes wide with fear; others hid amongst the pews, smearing themselves in blood from the already crimson floor. As machetes and hoes hacked towards me, I watched as one by one my entire family was butchered. My younger brother was the last to die. This once happy and mischievous little boy cried when our father was clubbed to death, revealing his hiding place under the altar; within seconds his small body was slashed to pieces. Amongst the killers, with whom we had lived side by side in the same community for years, was Sentwali, our neighbor. He knew our names; his children played with my younger brother in his garden; we had been welcomed into his home; we experienced his hospitality and now, someone whom we had considered not only our neighbor, but also our friend, had come to annihilate us.[60]

Desperate to Survive

During the period of the genocide, those Tutsis who had not yet been slain tried everything they could to save themselves. Often this entailed a grueling, agonizing, day-to-day struggle to find food and a place to sleep while evading the death squads. In many areas, those caught in this risky cycle spent the daylight hours hiding in forests, dense underbrush, or swamps. When darkness came, the killers usually departed to have supper and a good night's sleep. So the bedraggled fugitives left their hiding places long enough to find the supplies they needed to sustain themselves, then hid once again. A twenty-five-year-old farmer named Francine Niyitegeka later described how she survived by repeatedly moving in and out of a swamp:

[I] escaped into the bush. Among the trees I came upon a band of fugitives and we ran all the way to the marshes. I was to remain there for one month. Then we lived out days beyond misery. Each morning we went to hide the littlest ones beneath the swamp papyrus. Then we would sit on the dry grass and try to talk calmly together. When we heard the *Interahamwe* arrive, we ran to spread ourselves out in silence, in the thickest foliage, sinking deep into the mud. In the evening, when the killers had finished work and gone home, those who were not dead emerged from the marsh. The wounded simply lay down on the oozing bank of the bog, or in the forest. Those who still could went up to the school in [our town], to doze off in a dry place. And in the morning, quite early, we'd trudge down to go back into the marshes, covering the weakest among us with leaves to help them hide.[61]

Some of the other would-be victims of the death squads managed to survive through quite extraordinary means. Canadian physician James Orbinski, who did medical research and community service in Rwanda in the 1980s, interviewed a young girl whose family had been murdered by Hutu militiamen. Through an interpreter, the girl told

Whether it be in a forest, hut, marsh, or other structure, Tutsis would hide anywhere if it meant survival from the Hutu militia.

him, "My mother hid me in the latrines [deep, filthy pits used as toilets]. I saw through the hole [in the toilet seat]. I watched them hit her with machetes. I watched my mother's arm fall into my father's blood on the floor, and I cried without noise in the toilet."[62]

Another way that some Tutsis saved themselves was by telling convincing lies. They claimed they were not Tutsis, but rather Hutus who lived down the street, or had gotten lost, or were searching for relatives or friends. This ploy did not always work. But on occasion it did, as in the case of twelve-year-old Innocente Nyirahabimana. One day not long after the start of the mass killings, she came home from school and found several Hutu men armed with machetes hovering over her family members. It was clear that the intruders were about to murder them. They ordered Innocente to go stand with her relatives and prepare to die with them. Thinking quickly, however, she told them she was a Hutu neighbor who had been out for a walk and had wandered into the house out of curiosity. The Hutu killers believed her. Turning away from her, they proceeded to slaughter her relatives before her eyes. Later, as a young woman, she tearfully admitted, "I disowned my family to get a chance to survive."[63]

Human Decency and Courage

Incredibly, in the midst of the merciless slaughter of thousands of innocent people, there were also instances of human decency and courageous individuals who risked their lives to save others.

Some Hutus, for example, refused to descend into barbarism, as so many of their countrymen had. It has long been known that during World War II, several brave German families hid Jews in their homes to keep them safe from Nazi death squads. Likewise, during the Rwandan genocide, a number of Tutsis survived the slaughter because Hutu neighbors hid them from roving groups of militiamen and other killers. A Tutsi named Isaac Mugabe recalled:

> When our [Tutsi] neighbors were killed . . . we knew we would be next. Father sent me to a [Hutu] family friend named Ally Kamegeri. He hid me, along with the younger children, even though our parents couldn't come. He hid about 20 kids in total. That's how we lived until the end of genocide.[64]

The most famous example of such heroism and survival during the Rwandan crisis was Paul Rusesabagina's successful efforts to hide fugitives in the hotel he managed. He was born in 1954, the son of a Tutsi mother and a Hutu father. Despite the fact that the son was half Tutsi, he had long enjoyed protected status because he had business connections with several Hutu military officers.

When the mass killings began, Rusesabagina used his special status to good advantage. He allowed 1,268 Tutsis and moderate Hutus who had been marked for death to shelter themselves in the Sabena Hotel des Mille Collines, in Kigali. Because the facility had a capacity of only two hundred, conditions became extremely crowded and difficult. Rusesabagina recalls,

There was no water [except in the swimming pool, which people drank from], no electricity, and we were cooking any corn and dried beans we could find with firewood. But it's surprising how quickly people adapt to a situation, however

Paul Rusesabagina managed the Sabena Hotel des Mille Collines in Kigali. He sheltered 1,268 Tutsis and moderate Hutus from their would-be killers.

dangerous. Women were giving birth, young couples were getting married by a bishop from St. Michel Cathedral next door. . . . The hotel became a home, a lifestyle. People got used to sleeping in conference rooms and corridors.[65]

For seventy-eight days, the valiant and tireless Rusesabagina fended off repeated efforts by soldiers and other Hutu hard-liners to seize some or all of those he was protecting. Using a combination of his connections, impassioned verbal pleas, and most persuasive of all, hefty bribes, he kept the death squads at bay. Eventually he, his family, and all of the fugitives managed to flee to Tanzania.

Revenge or Healing?

Roughly three weeks after Rusesabagina's group made it to safety in Tanzania, the situation in Rwanda changed drastically. All during the massacres, the RPF fighters who had invaded from the north had made headway in their drive to capture the capital. The RPF contingent that had earlier been surrounded in Kigali had eventually broken out and joined up with the approaching main forces.

Finally in mid-July 1994 the combined rebel army entered Kigali in triumph. As the Hutu hard-liners who had been in power fled for Zaire, bordering Rwanda in the northwest, the Tutsi-dominated RPF set up an interim government. Its leaders ordered their troops to immediately put a stop to the genocide, which

"The Certainty of Death"

One of the many horrors of the Rwanda genocide was a waterfall choked with dead bodies. An unnamed witness recalls the sight:

The river Kagera flows into a steep ravine that forms the natural border between Tanzania and Rwanda. There is a small waterfall where the river narrows before entering the gorge. In the rainy season the river swells [and] gathers into its currents huge clumps of elephant grass and numerous small trees. In the late spring of 1994 it was much the same with human corpses. They, too, twisted and turned, rose, and dropped and came bouncing over the falls before they found the still water which would carry them down to Lake Victoria. They did not look dead. They looked like swimmers, because the strong currents invested them with powers of movement. So lifelike did they appear that for a few moments I winced as I watched them thrown against the rocks, imagining the pain they must be feeling. It was only beyond the falls, where they floated lifeless among the trees and grass, that one could accept the certainty of death.

Quoted in Peace Pledge Union, "Rwanda 1994: Witness." www.ppu.org.uk/genocide/g_rwanda3.html.

had gone on without interruption since early April.

People around the world now waited breathlessly to see what would happen next in Rwanda. Would the new government tell its soldiers to turn on and attack the Hutu population in an effort to get revenge for the slaughter of so many Tutsis? Or would order be restored and the people—Tutsis and Hutus alike—begin to heal the grievous wounds the country had recently sustained? It was clear that only time would tell.

Chapter Six

A Hopeful Future for All

The dramatic situation that existed in Rwanda directly after the end of the genocide is aptly described by a line from English poet John Milton's great epic, *Paradise Lost:* "Here the Archangel paused, betwixt the world destroyed and world restored."[66]

These words are indeed an appropriate metaphor for the exceptionally difficult state of affairs that the Rwandans faced in the late summer of 1994. It appeared to some foreign observers that the small African nation had virtually been destroyed, and decades would be required for it to recover from the genocide, if it ever did. Local hatreds were just too entrenched, they said, and the wounds suffered by the people too deep. Many thought Rwanda might well remain an unsafe and miserable place to live for a long time to come.

Others were more optimistic about the country's future. Many Rwandans were resilient, smart, and ethical, they

argued. Moreover, they had learned a big enough lesson from the tragedy to make it possible for them to rebound and restore their nation faster than the pessimists had predicted.

Fortunately for the country's people, a period of slow but steady recovery began. The new government called for peace and reconciliation (resolution of differences) between the former opposing national groups. Responding to this call, Rwanda began healing its psychological wounds, as well as rebuilding its shattered economy. That renewal continued and accelerated in the first decade of the twenty-first century. Recently, one outside observer called Rwanda "a new model of economic development."[67]

"People Can Be Changed"

The fact that Rwanda was in the midst of a resurgence fewer than two decades after the genocide was all the more impressive when one considers the scope of the human losses in the 1994 catastrophe. The exact number of people killed in the genocide is uncertain and may never be known. But there is no doubt that it was enormous by any standard. Estimates by various experts and investigative organizations range from 500,000 to 1 million deaths, with 800,000, give or take, being the most widely accepted and most-often cited figure.

People around the world were naturally horrified by the genocide in Rwanda and worried that acts of revenge by the new Tutsi government and army might be imminent. But such retaliation never occurred. Instead, the leaders of the new government, including RPF leader Paul Kagame, asked for all violence to stop and for order to be restored. Kagame and his chief supporters also called for all Rwandans, including the former murderers and their former victims, to try to patch up their differences. One official statement said:

> The Rwandan people were able to live together peacefully for six hundred years and there is no reason why they can't live together in peace again. Let me appeal to those who have chosen the murderous and confrontational path, by reminding them that they, too, are

A dying Rwandan woman breastfeeds her baby amid a sea of corpses in July 1994. To many outside observers it appeared the small African nation had been virtually destroyed.

Rwandans. Abandon your genocidal and destructive ways, join hands with other Rwandans, and put that energy to better use.[68]

This same diplomatic, constructive approach was also reflected in Rwanda's new leadership. Less than a year after the genocide, a coalition government, based to some degree on the one crafted in the Arusha Accords, formed. Over time it established new laws that banned discrimination on the basis of race, religion, or ethnic background. These statutes were a positive first step in creating an atmosphere of tolerance

Paul Kagami was elected president in August 1994 and immediately started the reconciliation process, calling for all Rwandans to reconcile their differences.

Scene from a refugee camp located in Zaire. Over 2 million Rwandans fled to neighboring countries to avoid the genocide.

in which all national parties and groups might steadily come together.

Partly because of these moderate, fairer policies, many of the more than 2 million Tutsis and Hutus who had fled before and during the genocide returned in the months and years that followed it. In 1996 and 1997 alone, more than a million refugees who had been living in neighboring countries went back to Rwanda. Among them were some of the former killers. Not surprisingly, this created numerous highly uncomfortable situations. Many of these individuals, after all, had been neighbors and coworkers of the people they had slain.

So tensions ran high when they returned to their villages and neighborhoods.

Hoping to lessen these tensions and thereby help the country heal itself, the government adopted a two-pronged approach to dealing with the former killers. This policy consisted of a mix of forgiveness and justice. It was widely seen as necessary from a practical standpoint because many hundreds of thousands of people had participated in the genocide. Most people recognized that it was unrealistic, if not impossible, to try to find and prosecute all of the killers. The more practical and sensible strategy seemed to be to try to forgive and/

Digging for Forensic Evidence

Clea Koff, a forensic anthropologist (an expert at identifying human remains), worked closely with the United Nations International Criminal Tribunal for Rwanda in the period following the genocide. In this passage from her book about her experiences there, she describes finding evidence of mass murders near a village church.

We spent days searching for surface skeletons, placing red flags in the soil as we worked until we had located so many that it was more helpful to ring whole areas in crime scene tape wrapped around tree trunks. Bones from multiple people were scattered across several meters through [natural] processes: mostly water runoff down the slope, but also disturbance by animals and perhaps by people, as they collected bananas and avocados from the trees. We recovered about fifty bones from the hillside and began analyzing them on tables we set up along one side of the church. . . . Anthropological analysis of the skeletons consisted of laying the bones out on the table in anatomical position, then determining age, sex, stature, and cause of death.

Clea Koff, *The Bone Woman: A Forensic Anthropologist's Search for Truth in the Mass Graves of Rwanda, Bosnia, Croatia, and Kosovo.* New York: Random House, 2004, p. 35.

or grant amnesty to many of those who had blindly followed the orders of the organizers and leaders of the massacres. Kagame justified this lenient, compassionate approach when he said, "People can be changed. Some people can even benefit from being forgiven, from being given another chance."[69]

Tribunals, Courts, and Justice

In spite of such enlightened principles and policies, achieving national reconciliation was not easy for many Rwandans. This was especially true for those who had lost loved ones in the massacres. One factor that helped them move forward with their lives, as well as begin to forgive, was the effort to bring the genocide's worst offenders, including its leaders, to justice. In 1996 the United Nations set up the International Criminal Tribunal for Rwanda (ICTR), a special court to deal with these mass murderers. After years on the run, Théoneste Bagosora, the genocide's chief architect, was captured and tried. In 2008 the ICTR found him guilty of multiple murders and sentenced him to life in prison. By 2010 the ICTR had convicted 29 of those charged as worst offenders; 11 trials were still in progress; 14 of the offenders were awaiting trial; and 13 were still at large.

Meanwhile, other wrongdoers were tried in Rwandan courts. Most of these operated on the local level and dealt with individuals charged with theft, murder, and other crimes committed in small communities during the genocide. The courts are part of the justice system known as Gacaca, in which members of a community elect local elders to act as judges.

Some of those convicted in these community courts went to prison. In December 2003, for example, eighteen people were found guilty of taking part in the large-scale massacre in Nyarubuye Church, in which five thousand to ten thousand people perished. One of those found guilty was sentenced to life in prison. (The death penalty was not an option because Rwanda had eliminated it years before.) Others who might have gotten life terms received sentences ranging from seven to sixteen years. They had their prison sentences reduced in return for public admissions of guilt. People charged with lesser crimes, such as theft, received even lighter, more merciful sentences, such as paying back the worth of the stolen goods or working in the fields of the victims' families. This flexible, tolerant approach to justice was another attempt by the new government to foster an atmosphere of reconciliation and national healing.

Lessons Learned?

In the years since the genocide, a number of concerned individuals and organizations asked if any lessons were learned

from it, and advised the major foreign governments to review their response to the crisis.

In that regard, the United States was one of the first nations to admit that it had not done enough to help Rwanda during its darkest hours. On March 25, 1998, President Clinton admitted that his country, like numerous other nations, had not tried hard enough to stop or at least reduce the scope of the violence. Therefore, those nations had to bear their share of responsibility for the tragedy. "We did not immediately call these crimes by their rightful name: genocide," he told a group of Rwandans during a visit to Kigali. "We cannot change the past. But we can and must do everything in our power to help you build a future without fear, and full of hope."[70]

Romeo Dallaire, the Canadian officer who had commanded the UN peacekeeping force in Rwanda, went further. He stated that there was only one effective way to avoid future calamities like the Rwandan genocide. This was for the residents of the developed (industrial or advanced) nations to learn to view all people, including those in third-world countries like Rwanda, as fully human and worth risking their own lives for. He added:

We in the developed world [often] act in a way that suggests we believe that our lives are worth more than the lives of other citizens of the planet. An American officer felt no shame as he informed me that the lives of 800,000 Rwandans were only worth risking the lives of ten American troops. The Belgians, after losing ten soldiers [in Rwanda], insisted that the lives of Rwandans were not worth risking another single Belgian soldier. The only conclusion I can reach is that we are in desperate need of a transfusion of humanity. If we believe that all humans are human . . . it can only be proven through [the] dollars we are prepared to expend to improve conditions in the Third World, [and] through the lives of our soldiers, which we are prepared to sacrifice for the sake of humanity.[71]

Former U.S. president Bill Clinton visits a Rwandan mass grave on July 23, 2005. Clinton admitted his country, as well as so many others, failed to stop or reduce the genocide.

Should the United States Intervene in Genocides?

Samantha Power, director of the Human Rights Initiative at the Kennedy School of Government at Harvard University in Cambridge, Massachusetts, here suggests that under certain conditions the American people might well have supported U.S. intervention in the Rwandan genocide.

American leaders say [that in staying out of situations like the Rwandan crisis] they are simply respecting the wishes of the American people, who have elected them, first and foremost, to fulfill the American dream of equality and freedom for all at home. Though this claim conforms with our intuitions and with the mounting data that the American public is becoming ever more isolationist, it may be misleading. . . . If American leaders ever used the word "genocide" to describe atrocities, it is likely that this public support would have grown. A July 1994 [poll] found that when [American] citizens were asked, "If genocidal situations occur, do you think that the UN, including the U.S., should intervene with whatever force is necessary to stop the acts of genocide," 65 percent said "always" or "in most cases," while 23 per cent said "only when American interests are also involved" and just 6 percent said "never." When asked how they would react if a UN commission decided that events in . . . Rwanda constituted genocide, 80 percent said they would favor intervention.

Samantha Power, "Never Again," www.pbs.org/wgbh/pages/frontline/shows/karadzic/genocide/neveragain.html.

Ambitious New Economic Goals

In the wake of the genocide and the inadequate response of so many nations, the leaders of Rwanda's government and business community realized that their third-world status was no longer acceptable. They had to do whatever was necessary to help the country's economy. But more than that, they needed to make Rwanda a place that both its citizens could be proud of and foreigners would want to trade with and invest in. Over time they developed some extremely ambitious economic goals. According to journalist Jeff Chu, Rwanda planned, among them

> to boost GDP [gross domestic product, the nation's overall economic output] sevenfold, find paying jobs for half of Rwanda's subsistence farmers, nearly quadruple per capita [annual] income to $900, and turn [the] country into an African center for technology, all by [the

year] 2020. The government [has been] doing what it can. It has, for instance, committed to investing annually 5% of its GDP in science and technology by 2012.[72]

These investments in science and technology were part of a larger effort by the new government, in league with members of the scientific and business communities, to undertake a major transformation of Rwanda's economy. The long-term plan was (and remains) to move from a largely agricultural economic base to one that mainly exploits technology. In particular, the aim was to introduce computers, broadband cables, and other devices that support information and knowledge-based technologies. The ultimate objective was to make Rwanda more competitive with European and other Western nations, as well as with successful Eastern nations, such as India and Japan.

No matter how motivated and hardworking the Rwandans might be, however, to achieve these challenging goals they also needed outside assistance. To this end, Rwanda vigorously sought to increase its trade relations with major foreign nations. Among the major trading partners the Rwandans dealt with in the late 1990s and beyond were Germany, Belgium, Uganda, and China.

In addition, Paul Kagame and other prominent Rwandans periodically met with the heads of large Western corporations. These companies included Costco and Starbucks, which rapidly became the world's biggest buyers of Rwandan coffee beans. Other large companies that decided to invest large sums in helping to develop Rwanda were Google, Real-Networks, and the Burlington Northern Santa Fe Railroad. The railroad company agreed to build a rail line linking Kigali with one of Tanzania's port towns along the shores of the Indian Ocean. Meanwhile RealNetworks, a digital entertainment company, supplied more than $6 million to build health centers in Rwanda. The company's founder and chief executive officer, Rob Glaser, said, "If we can make this place a beacon of hope, a place where just 15 years ago an eighth of the country was murdered in the most brutal way possible, then that hope should be possible anywhere."[73] These and similar large-scale economic activities helped to make Rwanda better known and respected among many nations outside of Africa.

Tourism and Popular Media

Another way that postgenocide Rwanda made itself known to people in other countries was through tourism and the popular media. In the late 1990s, tourism began to attract foreigners in increasing numbers. As this trend continued, tourism also became one of the country's most important local industries. A number of lakeside resorts became popular with foreign visitors, as did safaris to view the animals in Akagera National Park, near the border with Tanzania. In addition, many tourists started visiting one or more of several moving genocide memorials, including one dedicated to the Belgian soldiers who gave their lives

Don Cheadle portrays hero Paul Rusesabagina in the powerful 2004 film Hotel Rwanda *inspired by Rusesabagina's daring exploits during the mass murders.*

guarding Prime Minister Agathe Uwilingiyimana. The number-one tourist attraction, however, was, and remains, the habitats of Rwanda's mountain gorillas. Today several hundred people a month pay considerable sums to see these magnificent creatures up close.

Millions of people around the world who will never visit Rwanda personally learn about that country from popular media, especially from books and movies. Indeed, because the 1994 genocide constituted a human tragedy of uncommon size and horror, it was inevitable that it would later spawn books and movies. Among the best-selling books on the subject is Romeo Dallaire's powerful *Shake Hands with the Devil* (2003),

which chronicles his and his men's failed attempts to keep the peace during the turmoil. Also widely popular is journalist Philip Gourevitch's beautifully written account of the crisis, *We Wish to Inform You That Tomorrow We Will Be Killed with Our Families* (1998). It won numerous awards, including the Los Angeles Times Book Prize and the National Book Critics Circle Award.

Of the movies about Rwanda, none was more successful in introducing the country and the genocide to Western audiences than director Terry George's 2004 film *Hotel Rwanda*. Inspired by hotel manager Paul Rusesabagina's actions at the height of the genocide, the movie captures his courageous and successful attempt to save more than a thousand of his countrymen. Veteran American actor Don Cheadle, who portrays Rusesabagina, received an Oscar nomination for Best Actor. The film also won nominations for Best Supporting Actress and Best Screenplay, and the American Film Institute called it one of the one hundred most-inspirational movies of all time.

"People Are One"

One reason that George's film is so moving is that it stirringly depicts the feelings of hope that Rusesabagina and his companions harbored, despite their life-threatening predicament. While many of their neighbors sank into barbarism, they retained hope not only for themselves, but also for their war-torn country's future. The theme of a hopeful future has also been echoed by many Rwandans in the years since the genocide. In many parts of the country Tutsis and Hutus have come to live side by side in peace. That positive development has fostered cooperation and instilled a spark of confidence in the future in members of both groups. In April 2006 an elderly Rwandan named Tharcisse

Women Gain New Rights

The situation of many Rwandan women improved somewhat after the genocide. According to a postgenocide report by African Union, an international peacekeeping organization:

In the unwritten laws of Rwandan custom and tradition, women have been people of second-class status, leaving poor Rwandan women even worse off, as a group than poor Rwandan men. Although the Rwandan constitution guarantees women full legal equality, discrimination based on traditional practices has continued to govern many areas, including inheritance. At the time of the genocide, under customary law, a woman [only rarely could] inherit property. . . . As a result, many widows or daughters had no legal claim to the homes of their late husbands or fathers, or to their male relatives' land or bank accounts. After the genocide, a commission examined the situation and recommended ways to redress it, and the government subsequently introduced [laws] that would at last give women the right to own and inherit property.

African Union, "Rwanda: The Preventable Genocide," www.africa-union.org/official_documents/reports/Report_rowanda_genocide.pdf.

Mukama, who survived the genocide, fittingly captured that optimistic spark, saying,

I think things will get better, now that segregation no longer exists. In the past, we had our race written on our identity cards; first it said which clan a person belonged to, then later they changed it to race. Today, it has been removed; if things continue this way, they'll get better. We fight segregation today. People are one. Children are taught as one, taught the same things by the same teacher. If people are united at such an early stage, they will not become separated again. Division is created by bad leadership. The Rwandan government is fighting against segregation. This gives me hope.[74]

Notes

Introduction: A Crime Like No Other

1. Quoted in Alain Destexhe, "Rwanda and Genocide in the Twentieth Century," PBS, 1995. www.pbs.org/wgbh/pages/frontline/shows/rwanda/reports/dsetexhe.html.
2. Destexhe, "Rwanda and Genocide in the Twentieth Century."
3. "Charter of the International Military Tribunal: Nuremberg Trial Proceedings Vol. 1," Article 6c, Yale Law School Avalon Project. http://avalon.law.yale.edu/imt/judlawre.asp.
4. "Convention on the Prevention and Punishment of the Crime of Genocide," United Nations, December 9, 1948. www.hrweb.org/legal/genocide.html.
5. "Convention on the Prevention and Punishment of the Crime of Genocide."
6. Scott Straus, *The Order of Genocide: Race, Power, and War in Rwanda,* Ithaca, NY: Cornell University Press, 2006, p. 2.
7. Quoted in Jean Hatzfeld, *Life Laid Bare: The Survivors in Rwanda Speak,* New York: Other Press, 2000, p. 148.

Chapter One: Rwanda Before the Genocide

8. Quoted in "Get Facts About Rwanda," Rwanda Development Gateway. http://www.rwandagateway.org/spip.php?article89.
9. Quoted in Philip Gourevitch, *We Wish to Inform You That Tomorrow We Will Be Killed with Our Families: Stories from Rwanda,* New York: Farrar, Straus and Giroux, 1998, pp. 54–55.
10. Philip Briggs and Janice Booth. *Rwanda.* Guilford, CT: Globe Pequot Press, 2006, pp. 7–8.
11. Human Rights Watch, "History: The Meaning of 'Hutu,' 'Tutsi,' and 'Twa,'" www.hrw.org/legacy/reports/1999/rwanda/Geno1-3-09.htm#P200_83746.
12. Quoted in Tim Bewer et al., *West Africa,* Oakland, CA: Lonely Planet, p. 33.
13. Paul Rusesabagina with Tom Zoellner, *An Ordinary Man,* Thorndike, ME: Center Point, 2006, p. 46.
14. Rusesabagina, *An Ordinary Man,* p. 51.

Chapter Two: The Roots of Hatred

15. Straus, *The Order of Genocide,* pp. 19–20.
16. Rusesabagina, *An Ordinary Man,* p. 83.
17. Human Rights Watch, "History: The Meaning of 'Hutu,' 'Tutsi,' and 'Twa.'"

18. Straus, *The Order of Genocide*, pp. 20–21.
19. African Union, "Rwanda: The Preventable Genocide," African Union. www.africa-union.org/official_documents/reports/Report_rowanda_genocide.pdf.
20. Human Rights Watch, "History: The Transformation of 'Hutu' and 'Tutsi,'" www.hrw.org/legacy/reports/1999/rwanda/Geno1-3-09.htm#P200_83746.
21. Straus, *The Order of Genocide*, p. 22.
22. Human Rights Watch, "History: The Hutu Revolution," www.hrw.org/legacy/reports/1999/rwanda/Geno1-3-09.htm#P200_83746.
23. Briggs and Booth. *Rwanda*, p. 17.

Chapter Three: Power, Planning, and Propaganda

24. Quoted in Peace Pledge Union, "Rwanda 1994: Issues." www.ppu.org.uk/genocide/g_rwanda4.html.
25. Quoted in Gourevitch, *We Wish to Inform You That Tomorrow We Will Be Killed with Our Families*, p. 224.
26. Quoted in Human Rights Watch, "Choosing War: Hutu Power," www.hrw.org/legacy/reports/1999/rwanda/Geno1-3-11.htm#P638_245631.
27. Quoted in Human Rights Watch, "Choosing War."
28. Quoted in John A. Berry and Carol P. Berry, eds., *Genocide in Rwanda: A Collective Memory*, Washington, DC: Howard University Press, 1999, p. 113.
29. Human Rights Watch, "The Organization: Policitians and Militia," www.hrw.org/legacy/reports/1999/rwanda/Geno4-7-03.htm#P745_198290.
30. Quoted in Human Rights Watch, "The Organization."
31. Quoted in Jean Hatzfeld, *Machete Season: The Killers in Rwanda Speak*, New York: Farrar, Straus and Giroux, 2003, pp. 10–11.
32. Human Rights Watch, "Propaganda and Practice: The Media." www.hrw.org/legacy/reports/1999/rwanda/Geno1-3-10.htm#P419_175363.
33. Quoted in Rusesabagina, *An Ordinary Man*, p. 99.
34. Human Rights Watch, "Propaganda and Practice."
35. Straus, *The Order of Genocide*, p. 134.
36. Quoted in Genocide in Rwanda, "Propaganda: Tactics of Contradiction," www.trumanwebdesign.com/~catalina/analysis.htm.
37. Quoted in Genocide in Rwanda, "Propaganda."
38. Romeo Dallaire, *Shake Hands with the Devil: The Failure of Humanity in Rwanda*, New York: Carroll and Graf, 2003, p. 123.
39. Quoted in Dallaire, *Shake Hands with the Devil*, p. 128.

Chapter Four: The Butchery Begins

40. Dallaire, *Shake Hands with the Devil*, p. 142.
41. Romeo Dallaire, "Outgoing Coded Cable: January 11, 1994," PBS. www.pbs.org/wgbh/pages/frontline/shows/evil/warning/cable.html.
42. Kofi Annan, "The UN's Response: January 11, 1994," PBS. www.pbs.org/wgbh/pages/frontline/

shows/evil/warning/unresponse.html.

43. Dallaire, *Shake Hands with the Devil*, p. 146.

44. Human Rights Watch, "April 1994: 'The Month That Would Not End'; The Attack on Habyarimana's Plane. www.hrw.org/legacy/reports/1999/rwanda/Geno4-7-02.htm#P406_90150.

45. Straus, *The Order of Genocide*, p. 47.

46. Rusesabagina, *An Ordinary Man*, p. 119.

47. Peace Pledge Union, "Rwanda 1994: The Genocide." www.ppu.org.uk/genocide/g_rwanda1.html.

48. Quoted in Gourevitch, *We Wish to Inform You That Tomorrow We Will Be Killed with Our Families*, p. 113.

49. Quoted in PBS, "100 Days of Slaughter: A Chronology of U.S./U.N. Actions," PBS, www.pbs.org/wgbh/pages/frontline/shows/evil/etc/slaughter.html.

50. Quoted in PBS. "100 Days of Slaughter."

51. Human Rights Watch, "The Genocide," www.hrw.org/legacy/reports/1999/rwanda/Geno1-3-02.htm#P21_7273.

Chapter Five: The Genocide at Its Height

52. Quoted in Hatzfeld, *Life Laid Bare*, p. 51.

53. Human Rights Watch, "The Genocide."

54. Gourevitch, *We Wish to Inform You That Tomorrow We Will Be Killed with Our Families*, p. 115.

55. Quoted in Hatzfeld, *Machete Season*, pp. 73–74.

56. Quoted in Straus, *The Order of Genocide*, p. 74.

57. Quoted in Hatzfeld, *Machete Season*, p. 50.

58. Quoted in Hatzfeld, *Machete Season*, pp. 47–48.

59. Quoted in Rakiya Omaar et al., *Rwanda: Death, Despair, and Defiance*, Kigali, Rwanda: African Rights, 1994, pp. 403–404.

60. Lucy Hall, "Massacre at Nyarubuye: The Story of Survivor Rosine Nshirmiriama," Century of Genocide Exhibition Project. www.centuryofgenocide.com/exhibition/page48/page91/page91.html.

61. Quoted in Hatzfeld, *Life Laid Bare*, p. 37.

62. Quoted in James Orbinski, *An Imperfect Offering: Humanitarian Action for the Twenty-First Century*, New York: Walker, 2008, p. 10.

63. Quoted in James Estrin, "They Survived the Rwandan Genocide," Lens (blog), March 25, 2010. http://lens.blogs.nytimes.com/2010/03/25/showcase-143.

64. Issac Mugabe, "An Orphan's Story of Survival and Hope for the Future." http://rwandansurvivors.blogspot.com, March 21, 2006.

65. Quoted in *O, The Oprah Magazine*, "Oprah Talks to Paul Rusesabagina," March 1, 2006, www.oprah.com/omagazine/Oprah-Talks-To-Paul-Rusesabagina/3.

Chapter Six: A Hopeful Future for All

66. Quoted in Gourevitch, *We Wish to Inform You That Tomorrow We Will Be Killed with Our Families*, p. 175;

for the line in its original context, see "Paradise Lost: The Twelfth Book," Bartleby.com. www.bartleby .com/4/412.html.

67. Jeff Chu, "Rwanda Rising: A New Model of Economic Development," Fast Company, April 1, 2009. www .fastcompany.com/magazine/134/ special-report-rwanda-rising.html.

68. Quoted in Peace Pledge Union, "Rwanda 1994: After the Genocide." www.ppu.org.uk/genocide/g_ rwanda2.html.

69. Quoted in Peace Pledge Union, "Rwanda 1994: After the Genocide."

70. Quoted in PBS, "100 Days of Slaughter."

71. Dallaire, *Shake Hands with the Devil*, p. 522.

72. Chu, "Rwanda Rising."

73. Quoted in Chu, "Rwanda Rising."

74. Tharcisse Mukama, "About the History of Segregation and Resulting Conflict in Rwanda." http://rwandan survivors.blogspot.com, April 6, 2006.

For More Information

Books

Romeo Dallaire, *Shake Hands with the Devil: The Failure of Humanity in Rwanda*. New York: Carroll and Graf, 2003. The gripping story of how the commander of the United Nations forces in Rwanda and his men saved many lives but were unable to rally world support for their efforts.

Alison Des Forges, *Leave None to Tell the Story: Genocide in Rwanda*. New York: Human Rights Watch and International Federation of Human Rights, 1999. This book is widely seen as the most authoritative survey of the horrifying tragedy in Rwanda.

Philip Gourevitch, *We Wish to Inform You That Tomorrow We Will Be Killed with Our Families: Stories from Rwanda*. New York: Farrar, Straus and Giroux, 1998. This award-winning, riveting book describes the complex background of the genocide, as well as the event itself and its aftermath.

Jean Hatzfeld, *Life Laid Bare: The Survivors in Rwanda Speak*. New York: Other Press, 2000. Hatzfeld presents several moving eyewitness accounts by survivors of the genocide.

Jean Hatzfeld, *Machete Season: The Killers in Rwanda Speak*. New York: Farrar, Straus and Giroux, 2003. A compilation of first-person narratives by some of the Rwandans who took part in the mass killings.

David C. King, *Rwanda*. New York: Marshall Cavendish, 2007. In language aimed at teens, this nicely illustrated book provides information on Rwanda's geography, population, economy, history, and more.

Clea Koff, *The Bone Woman: A Forensic Anthropologist's Search for Truth in the Mass Graves of Rwanda, Bosnia, Croatia, and Kosovo*. New York: Random House, 2004. This book describes a scientist's efforts to gather evidence to prosecute the perpetrators of the Rwandan genocide.

Andy Koopmans, *Rwanda*. Philadelphia: Mason Crest, 2005. This book for young people tells how the Rwandan genocide came about, including the animosity between the Hutus and Tutsis.

James Orbinski, *An Imperfect Offering: Humanitarian Action for the Twenty-First Century*. New York: Walker, 2008. The genocide in Rwanda is one of several perilous situations worldwide that Orbinski, formerly of Doctors Without Borders, expertly chronicles in this book.

Paul Rusesabagina with Tom Zoellner, *An Ordinary Man*. Thorndike, ME: Center Point, 2006. This moving book is about a local hotel manager who saved many people from death in the Rwandan genocide.

Scott Straus, *The Order of Genocide: Race, Power, and War in Rwanda*. Ithaca, NY: Cornell University Press, 2006. Straus ably traces the genocide and analyzes its political and social dimensions.

Internet Sources

BBC, "Rwanda: How the Genocide Happened," BBC. http://news.bbc.co.uk/2/hi/1288230.stm.

Human Rights Watch, "The Rwandan Genocide: How It Was Prepared," Human Rights Watch, April 2006. www.hrw.org/backgrounder/africa/rwanda0406.

Peace Pledge Union, "Genocides: Rwanda 1994," www.ppu.org.uk/genocide/g_rwanda.html.

Television Documentaries

"The Triumph of Evil," *Frontline*, Arlington, VA: PBS, January 26, 1999. www.pbs.org/wgbh/pages/frontline/shows/evil. A brief but informative synopsis of the massacre, with several links to other international cases of genocide.

"Rwanda: How the Genocide Happened," BBC. http://news.bbc.co.uk/2/hi/1288230.stm. A well-written short overview of the tragedy.

"The Rwandan Genocide: How It was Prepared," Human Rights Watch. http://www.hrw.org/backgrounder/africa/rwanda0406/. An excellent general account of the event, with much useful analysis of political, social, economic, ethnic, and other factors.

Index

Germany
colonization of Rwanda, 21–22
Nazi, 9–10
Goebbels, Joseph, 48, *48*
Gorillas, mountain, 18, *18*
Götzen, Gustav Adolf von, 21
Gourevitch, Philip, 72, 87

H
Habyarimana, Juvénal, 26, *34*,
34–35, 53
assassination of, 56–57, 63
forms coalition government, 37
rallies support against Tutsis,
36
Hamitic theory, 31
Hill, Maranyunda, 12
Holocaust, 9
Hotel Rwanda (film), 87–88
Human Rights Watch
on anti-Tutsi propaganda, 47, 49
on Habyarimana assassination,
57–58
on Hutu Revolution, 33
on incentives for militias, 67–68
on Kingdom of Rwanda, 19–20,
28–29
on racism fostered by Belgians/
Catholic Church, 31–32
Hutu Power, 39, 41–42
Hutu Revolution (1959–1961), 33
Hutu Ten Commandments, 42
Hutu(s), 16
emancipation movement, 24
interventions to save Tutsis by,
75

militias, 45–46, *46*
opposition to Arusha Accords
among, 38
origin of term, 28–29
as percent of Rwandan
population, 28

I
ICTR (International Criminal
Tribunal for Rwanda), 82
Interahamwe (youth militia),
45–46, 74
motivations of, 67–68
as trained to massacre, 62
International Criminal Tribunal
for Rwanda (ICTR), 82

J
Jean-Pierre (informant), 54

K
Kagame, Paul, 79, *80*, 82, 86
Kangura (newspaper), 42
Karamira, Froduald, *41*,
41–42
Kayibanda, Gregiore, 24, *25*,
25–26, 33
Kigali massacres, 59–60

L
Lacger, Louis de, 16–17
Lake Muhazi, 17
League of Nations, 23

Lemkin, Raphael, 10
Leopold II (king of Belgium), 21, 22

M
Militias. *See* Interahamwe
Milton, John, 78
Mount Karisimbi, 15, *15*
Mugabe, Isaac, 75
Mugesera, Leon, 49, *50*
Mukama, Tharcisse, 88–89
Munyaneza, Janvier, 66
Mutara III (Rwandan king), 24
Mutungirehe, Pio, 69–70

N
National Revolutionary
   Movement for Development,
   34
Nazi Germany, 9–10, 48
Ndori, Ruganzu, 19
Ngeze, Hassan, 42, 43, *43*
Niyitegeka, Francine, 73–74
Nkinamubanzi, Anatase, 70
Nshirmiriama, Rosine, 73
Ntaromira, Cyprien, 57, 63
Nuremberg Trials (1945), 11
Nyiginya clan, 19
Nyirahabimana, Innocente, 75
Nzirorera, Joseph, 58

O
Organization of African Union,
   31

P
Pan-African movement, 24
Paradise Lost (Milton), 78
Pinsky, Helene, 52
Pol Pot, 11
Power, Samantha, 85

R
Radio
   anti-Tutsi propaganda on,
      42, 47, 49–50
   Nazi propaganda on, 48
   orders to death squads
      given by, 61
RPF. *See* Rwandan Patriotic
   Front
Ruanda-Urundi, 21, 23
   division of, 25
Rusesabagina, Paul, 27–28, 51,
   75–76, *76*, 88
Rwanda
   under Belgian rule, 23–24
   climate of, 13, 15–16
   under dictatorship of
      Habyarimana, 34–35
   early history, 16–17
   economic goals of, 85–86
   German colonization of,
      21–22
   independence of, 24–26
   Kingdom of, 17, 19–20
   map of, *14*
   physical features of, 13, 15
   population breakdown of,
      28

About the Author

In addition to his acclaimed volumes on the ancient world, historian Don Nardo has written and edited many books for young adults about modern history, including *The Atlantic Slave Trade*, *The Age of Colonialism*, *The Great Depression*, *World War II in the Pacific*, a four-volume survey of the Industrial Revolution, and biographies of Adolf Hitler and Franklin D. Roosevelt. Mr. Nardo also writes screenplays and teleplays and composes orchestral music. He lives with his wife, Christine, in Massachusetts.

Picture Credits

Cover: © Marcin Jamkowski/ Adventure Pictures/Alamy

AFP/Getty Images, 6, 9

AP Images/Chris Tomlinson, 41

AP Images/Jacques Boissinot, 50

AP Images/Jim Collins, 7

AP Images/Jean Marc Boujou, 7, 46, 71

AP Images/Michael Lipchitz, 6

© Arts & Authors/Alamy, 76

© Bettmann/Corbis, 25, 29

© Charles Caratini/Sygma/Corbis, 81

© Corinne Dufka/Reuters/Corbis, 57, 79

© Craig Lovell/Eagle Visions Photography/Alamy, 18

Derrick Ceyrac/AFP/Getty Images, 34

Fox Photos/Getty Images, 48

Galerie Bilderwelt/Hulton Archive/ Getty Images, 11

Hulton Archive/Getty Images, 32

Jose Cendon/AFP/Getty Images, 84

Kennedy Ndahiro/AFP/Getty Images, 38

© Last Refuge/Alamy, 15

Mansell/Time Life Pictures/Getty Images, 6

Martin & Osa Johnson Archive/Getty Images, 17

© Mary Evans Picture Library, 22

Olinchuck/www.shutterstock.com, 14

© Orban Thierry/Sygma/Corbis, 67

© Pascal Le Segretain/Sygma/Corbis, 59

© Patrick Robert/Sygma/Corbis, 36

© Photo12/Alamy, 87

© Roger Tidman/Corbis, 20

© Sam Kiley/Sygma/Corbis, 61, 72, 74

Scott Peterson/Getty Images, 55, 60, 64

Stella Vuzo/AFP/Getty Images, 43

Walter Dhladhla/AFP/Getty Images, 80

W

We Wish to Inform You That Tomorrow We Will be Killed With Our Families (Gourevitch), 72, 87

Wilheim II (German Kaiser), 23

World War I, 22–23

Y

Youth militias. *See* Interahamwe

Yuhi IV (Rwandan king), 24

Z

Zaire, *81*